AF326508

Systematic Theology for Teens

*A Clear Guide to What Christians Believe
and Why It Matters*

TABLE OF CONTENTS

INTRODUCTION
WHY WHAT YOU BELIEVE CHANGES EVERYTHING

You make hundreds of choices every single day. You decide what to wear when you get up. You choose which friends to sit with at lunch. You pick which videos to watch or which games to play. Most of these choices feel small. They do not seem to change your life much. But under these small choices are much bigger ones.

You have views about who you are. You have ideas about right and wrong. You have thoughts about where the world came from and where it is going. These big ideas are like the OS on your phone. You might not see the code, but it runs every app you use. If the code is broken, the phone does not work right.

This book is about that "code." We are going to look at what Christians believe and why those beliefs matter. This is not just for people who want to be pastors. This is for you.

What Is Systematic Theology?

The name of this book is a bit of a mouthful. Let's break it down into simple terms.

Theology comes from two Greek words. *Theos* means "God" and *logos* means "word" or "study." So, theology is simply the study of God. It is the effort to know who God is and what He has done. If you have ever thought about God or asked a question about Him, you were doing theology.

Systematic means organized. Think about a library. If all the books were thrown in a giant pile in the middle of the floor, you would never find what you need. A library is helpful because it is organized. History is in one spot. Science is in another.

Systematic Theology is just an organized way of looking at the Bible. Instead of reading from page one to the end, we pick a topic. We look at everything the Bible says about that topic from start to finish. We put those truths together so we can see the whole picture clearly.

Why Does This Matter for You?

Some people think that "doctrine" or "theology" is boring. They think it is just for old books and dusty classrooms. They might say, "I just want to love Jesus. I don't need all that technical stuff."

But you cannot love someone you do not know. If you say you love your best friend but you think they are a 50-year-old man from Alaska when they are actually a 15-year-old girl from your town, you don't really love *them*. You love a version of them you made up.

Knowing the truth about God is the only way to love the real God. Here are three reasons why this study is vital:

- **It protects you from lies.** Plenty of people will tell you who God is. Some say He is a mean judge. Others say He is a cosmic Santa Claus who just wants you to be happy. Theology helps you compare those ideas to the Bible.

- **It gives you a solid foundation.** Life can get messy. Friends walk away. Grades drop. People get sick. If your faith is based only on a "feeling," it will shake when things go wrong. Knowing the character of God gives you a rock to stand on.

- **It leads to right living.** What you think about God changes how you treat people. It changes how you use your money and your time. Clear thinking leads to a life that honors Him.

"Do not conform to the pattern of this world, but be transformed by the renewing of your mind. Then you will be able to test and approve what God's will is—his good, pleasing and perfect will." - *Romans 12:2*

A God-Centered Approach

Many books for teens focus on "you." They talk about your dreams, your problems, and your potential. While those things matter, they are not the main point of the Bible.

The Bible is a book about God.

In this book, we will start with God. We will look at His nature, His plan, and His work. When you see how big and good God is, your own life starts to make sense. You find your value because He made you. You find your purpose because He called you. You find your hope because He saved you.

We will use the Bible as our primary tool. We believe that God has spoken clearly in His Word. We do not have to guess what He is like. He told us.

What to Expect

We have organized this guide into sections. Each part builds on the one before it. We will start with the Bible itself. Then we will look at God the Father, the problem of sin, and the work of Jesus. We will finish by looking at the church and what happens at the end of time.

As you read, you might find some ideas that are new to you. You might find things that are hard to grasp at first. That is okay. God is infinite. We are not. We should expect to find things about Him that are bigger than our own brains.

This is not a book you have to rush through. Take your time. Think about the verses. Ask God to help you see the truth. The goal is not just to finish the book. The goal is to know the Creator of the universe.

To get the most value out of these pages, try the following:

1. **Read with a Bible nearby.** Do not just take my word for it. Look up the verses yourself.

2. **Ask questions.** If something is confusing, talk to a parent, a youth leader, or a pastor.

3. **Apply it.** Every chapter ends with a section on why the topic matters. Do not skip this. Theology is meant to be lived, not just filed away.

Knowledge of God is the greatest treasure you can have. It is better than a high GPA, a big bank account, or a lot of followers. When you know who God is, you know the truth that sets you free.

Let's begin.

PART ONE

THE FOUNDATION

CHAPTER 1

THE BOOK GOD WROTE (THE BIBLE)

Imagine you are walking through a thick forest. The trees are tall, and the brush is so dense you can barely see your own feet. You have no map and no cell service. You feel lost. Suddenly, you look down and see a clear, well-lit path. Even better, there is a guide waiting for you who knows every inch of the woods. He has a letter for you that explains exactly how to get home.

Life often feels like that forest. You face big questions about your future, your identity, and what is true. You do not have to guess the answers. God did not leave us to wander in the dark. He spoke. He gave us a book to show us who He is and how we should live. We call this book the Bible.

God Is Not Silent

The most important thing to know about God is that He wants to be known. He is not a distant force hiding behind the clouds. He is a person who communicates. In theology, we use the word **revelation** to describe God showing Himself to us.

Think about meeting a new person. You can look at their clothes or their hair to learn a little bit about them. But you will never really know their heart until they speak to you. God has "spoken" to us in two main ways.

1. The World Around Us (General Revelation)

God speaks through what He made. When you look at a sunset or the vastness of the ocean, you see His power. When you look at the tiny details of a leaf or the human eye, you see His wisdom. The stars tell us that God is great.

This is called "general" because it is available to everyone, everywhere. You do not need a Bible to see that a Creator exists. Psalm 19:1 says, "The heavens declare the glory of God, and the sky above proclaims his handiwork." Nature is like a giant billboard pointing to God.

2. The Word of God (Special Revelation)

Nature tells us God is powerful, but it does not tell us His name. It does not tell us how He feels about sin or how we can be saved. For that, we need "special" revelation. This is where God uses words.

God spoke through prophets. He spoke through His Son, Jesus. And He gave us the Bible so we would have a permanent record of His truth. The Bible is God's specific message to us.

Where Did the Bible Come From?

If you look at the Bible, you will see it is a big book made of 66 smaller books. It was written by about 40 different men over a span of 1,500 years. These men were kings, farmers, doctors, and fishermen. They wrote in different languages and lived in different countries.

Yet, when you read the Bible, it tells one single, perfect story. It does not contradict itself. How is that possible?

The answer is **inspiration**.

> "All Scripture is God-breathed and is useful for teaching, rebuking, correcting and training in righteousness," - *2 Timothy 3:16*

When the Bible says Scripture is "breathed out" by God, it means He is the ultimate source. The human authors were not like robots. God did not put them in a trance and take over their hands. They used their own styles and personalities. But the Holy Spirit guided them so perfectly that every word they wrote was exactly what God wanted to say.

Because God is the real author, the Bible is different from any other book on your shelf. It is not just a collection of human ideas. It is the Word of the Living God.

Can We Trust It?

Since God is perfect and cannot lie, His Word is perfect too. We use the word **inerrancy** to describe this. It means the Bible, in its original form, does not have any errors. It is completely true in everything it teaches.

Some people might tell you the Bible is just full of myths. But the more we learn about history and archaeology, the more the Bible is proven right. It describes real people, real places, and real events.

Even more importantly, the Bible is **sufficient**. This means it gives us everything we need to know for a life of faith. We do not need new messages or "secret" codes. If we want to know what God thinks about a topic, we look at the Bible. It is the final authority for what we believe and how we act.

The Purpose of the Bible

God did not give us the Bible just so we could win a trivia game. He gave it to us to change us.

- **It shows us our need.** The Bible is like a mirror. It shows us our sin and our need for a Savior.

- **It points to Jesus.** From the first page to the last, the Bible is about God's plan to rescue us through Christ.

- **It guides our steps.** Psalm 119:105 says, "Your word is a lamp to my feet and a light to my path." It helps us make wise choices in a confusing world.

- **It feeds our souls.** Just as your body needs food to grow, your spirit needs the Word of God to stay healthy.

How to Approach the Bible

Since the Bible is God's Word, we should treat it with respect. It is not a book you read once and put away. It is a book you live in.

Try to read it every day. You do not have to read five chapters at a time. Even a few verses can give you something to think about all day. When you read, ask God to help you see what He wants to show you.

Do not be discouraged if some parts are hard to understand. Some parts of the Bible are like deep water. You can keep swimming in them for your whole life and still find new things. The main message, however, is clear: God loves us, we are sinners, and Jesus is the way home.

Why This Matters to You

What you think about the Bible changes how you hear God. If the Bible is just a human book, you can pick and choose which parts to follow. You can ignore the parts that are hard or the parts you do not like.

But if the Bible is the Word of God, it has authority over your life. When you read it, you are listening to your Creator. You can trust it when you are sad. You can lean on it when you are afraid. You can build your whole life on its promises, and you will never be let down.

Knowing that God wrote a book for you is a beautiful thing. It means you are never truly lost. You have a guide. You have a map. You have the truth.

Reflect and Talk

1. If the Bible is "breathed out" by God, how should that change the way you feel when you open it?

2. Have you ever felt like nature was "speaking" to you about God? What did it say?

3. What is one area of your life where you need the Bible to be a "lamp to your feet" right now?

CHAPTER 2

IS THE BIBLE TRUE?

It is one thing to say the Bible is God's Word. It is another thing to believe it when your friends, your teachers, or people on the internet say it is a book of fairytales. Maybe you have sat in your room and wondered, *How do I really know this is true?* Asking questions is not a sign of weak faith. God is not afraid of your questions. He made your mind, and He wants you to use it. We do not have to check our brains at the door to believe the Bible. In fact, the more we look at the evidence, the more we see that the Bible is the most reliable book in history.

The Amazing Puzzle

In the last chapter, we mentioned that the Bible has about 40 authors. Think about that for a second. Imagine you gathered 40 people from different countries. Some are from the 1800s, some from the 1900s, and some from today. They speak different languages. They have different jobs.

Now, ask each of them to write one chapter of a book about the meaning of life. If you put those chapters together, what would you get? You would get a mess. The writers would disagree on almost everything.

But the Bible is different. Even though it was written over 1,500 years by men who often never met, it tells one unified story. It has one clear theme: God's plan to rescue people through Jesus. Every "piece" of the puzzle fits perfectly. This unity is a miracle. It shows that one Mind was behind the whole thing.

One of the best ways to know if someone is telling the truth is to see if they keep their promises. The Bible is full of **prophecies**. These are moments where God told people what would happen hundreds of years before it took place.

If a psychic predicts that it will rain tomorrow, that is a guess. If a prophet predicts that a specific person will be born in a specific town and die in a specific way 700 years later, that is God.

The Old Testament contains hundreds of these details about Jesus.

- **His Birth:** Micah 5:2 said He would be born in Bethlehem.
- **His Rejection:** Isaiah 53 said His own people would turn against Him.
- **His Death:** Psalm 22 described His hands and feet being pierced long before the Romans even invented crucifixion.

The odds of one man fulfilling just eight of these prophecies by chance are nearly impossible. Jesus fulfilled all of them. God used these "receipts" to prove that His Word is true.

The Dirt Does Not Lie

Some people think the Bible is just a book of myths like the stories of Greek gods. But myths usually happen in "a land far, far away" at an unknown time. The Bible is different. It names real cities, real kings, and real dates.

For a long time, some critics said the Bible was wrong about certain groups of people, like the Hittites. They claimed the Hittites never existed. Then, in the early 1900s, archaeologists dug into the dirt and found the ruins of the Hittite capital. They found their records and their art. The Bible was right all along.

We also have the **Dead Sea Scrolls**. These are ancient copies of the Bible found in caves in 1947. They are over 2,000 years old. When scholars compared these ancient scrolls to the Bibles we have today, they were almost identical. This proves that the Bible has not been changed or corrupted over time. God has preserved His message.

The Witness of Jesus

If you want to know if the Bible is true, look at what Jesus thought. Jesus is the center of our faith. He rose from the dead, which proves He is who He said He is.

When Jesus was on earth, He quoted the Bible constantly. He called it "the commandment of God." He treated the stories of Adam and Eve, Noah, and Jonah as real history. He never corrected the Bible. Instead, He used it to defeat the devil and to teach His followers.

If we trust Jesus with our lives, we should trust the book He loved. He believed every word was true.

The Power to Change Lives

There is one more kind of evidence that is very personal. It is the evidence of a changed life.

No other book has the power that the Bible has. Millions of people throughout history have been changed by its words.

- It has turned angry people into kind leaders.
- It has given hope to people who wanted to give up.
- It has given peace to people in the middle of wars.

When you read the Bible, it does not just give you information. It speaks to your heart. It tells you the truth about yourself, even the parts you try to hide. Then it shows you the grace of God that covers those parts. You can know the Bible is true because you can see it working in the world and in your own soul.

> "The law of the Lord is perfect, refreshing the soul. The statutes of the Lord are trustworthy, making wise the simple." - *Psalm 19:7*

Faith and Facts

Does this mean we have every single answer? No. There are still things in history we are learning. There are still passages that are hard to understand.

But faith is not "blind." Blind faith is believing in something when there is no reason to. Biblical faith is trusting in God because He has shown Himself to be trustworthy. We have enough evidence to know that the Bible is a solid foundation. You can build your life on it without being afraid that it will crack.

Why This Matters to You

If the Bible is just a book of opinions, you do not have to listen to it. You can do whatever feels right in the moment. You can follow the crowd or do what is popular on social media.

But if the Bible is true, you have an anchor. When the world feels chaotic and everyone is shouting different "truths," you have the real Truth.

- You don't have to wonder if you matter; God says you do.
- You don't have to wonder if there is hope for the world; God says there is.
- You don't have to guess how to live a good life; God has given you the map.

Believing the Bible is true gives you a confidence that nothing else can. It means that when you open your Bible, you aren't just reading ancient history. You are hearing from the Creator who knows you by name.

Reflect and Talk

1. Which piece of evidence, unity, prophecy, archaeology, or changed lives, is most helpful to you when you have doubts?
2. Why is it important that the Bible mentions real places and real people instead of being a "long time ago in a galaxy far away"?
3. If you really believed the Bible was 100% true, how would that change the way you read it tomorrow morning?

PART TWO

THE CREATOR

CHAPTER 3

WHO IS GOD?

If you want to know what someone is like, you look at their actions. You listen to their words. You see how they treat others. Learning about God is no different. But there is one big problem. God is much bigger than we are. Trying to understand God is a bit like an ant trying to understand how the internet works. The ant can see the router and feel the warmth of the wires. But it cannot grasp the code or the vast network behind it.

Thankfully, God has not left us guessing. He has told us about His character. In this chapter, we will look at who God is. We will see that He is not just a "force" or a "vibe." He is a living Person with specific traits. These traits tell us that He is worthy of our trust and our worship.

God Is Spirit and He Is One

Before we look at what God *does*, we have to look at what God *is*. The Bible tells us: "God is spirit, and his worshipers must worship in the Spirit and in truth." (John 4:24). This means He does not have a physical body like we do. He is not made of skin, bones, or atoms. Because He is spirit, He is not limited by space or time. He does not get tired. He does not need to sleep or eat.

The Bible also teaches that there is only one God. This is called **monotheism**. In the ancient world, people worshipped hundreds of different gods. They had a god for the sun, a god for the rain, and a god for the crops. But the Bible is clear: "The Lord our God, the Lord is one" (Deuteronomy 6:4). Everything in the universe was made by this one Creator.

God Has a Name

God is not just a title. He has a personal name. In the Old Testament, God revealed His name to Moses as **Yahweh**. In English, we often translate this as "The LORD" (in all capital letters).

The name Yahweh means "I Am Who I Am." It tells us that God is self-existent. He does not need anything from us. He did not need to be created. He has always been there, and He will always be there. He is the source of all life. When we call on God, we are calling on a Person who is completely independent and eternal.

Attributes You Cannot Share

Theologians often split God's traits into two groups. The first group includes things that are true *only* of God. No human can ever have these traits. These help us see how great He is.

1. God Knows Everything (Omniscience)

God has never learned a new fact. He has never had an "aha!" moment. He knows everything that has happened, everything that is happening, and everything that will ever happen. He even knows your secret thoughts and your future choices. Psalm 139:4 says, "Even before a word is on my tongue, behold, O Lord, you know it altogether."

2. God Is Everywhere (Omnipresence)

There is no place you can go where God is not present. He is in the highest heaven and the deepest ocean. He is with you in your bedroom and He is with a believer on the other side of the planet at the exact same time. This does not mean God *is* the trees or the rocks. It means He is present everywhere in His creation.

3. God Is All-Powerful (Omnipotence)

God can do anything that is consistent with His character. He created the entire universe out of nothing just by speaking. He sustains the stars and keeps the planets in orbit. There is no problem in your life that is too big for Him. Nothing is too hard for the Lord.

4. God Never Changes (Immutability)

The world changes every day. Fashion changes. Technology changes. Even your best friends might change. But God never changes. His character, His promises, and His truth are the same today as they were thousands of years ago. You can count on Him because: "Every good and perfect gift is from above, coming down from the Father of the heavenly lights, who does not change like shifting shadows." (James 1:17).

Attributes You Can Reflect

The second group of traits includes things that God has, but that we can also have (in a much smaller way). God made us in His image, so we can reflect these parts of His character.

- **God is Holy:** To be "holy" means to be set apart or "cut off" from everything else. God is perfectly pure. There is no sin in Him. He is the standard for what is good and right.

- **God is Just:** God always does what is right. He is a perfect Judge. He cannot ignore sin, and He will make sure that justice is done in the end. He is fair in all His ways.

- **God is Love:** This is not just something God does; it is who He is. His love is not a "crush" or a feeling that comes and goes. It is a steady, sacrificial commitment to the good of others. He showed this most clearly by sending Jesus to die for us.

- **God is Truth:** God is the source of all truth. He cannot lie. Everything He says is a perfect match for reality. You can trust His Word because it is impossible for Him to be wrong.

  "Each of the four living creatures had six wings and was covered with eyes all around, even under its wings. Day and night they never stop saying: "'Holy, holy, holy is the Lord God Almighty, who was, and is, and is to come.'" - *Revelation 4:8*

Why This Matters to You

Knowing who God is changes how you see your daily life. If God were just a powerful force, you might be afraid of Him. If He were just a loving friend, you might not respect Him. But because He is both great and good, you can rest.

When you feel lonely, remember His omnipresence. You are never truly alone. The Creator of the stars is right there in the room with you.

When you feel confused, remember His omniscience. You do not have to have all the answers for your life. God already knows the path ahead. He is not surprised by the things that surprise you.

When you feel guilty, remember His holiness and His love. His holiness shows you that your sin is serious. But His love tells you that He has provided a way for you to be forgiven and brought back to Him.

When the world feels out of control, remember His omnipotence and immutability. Politicians may fail and the economy may crash. But the God who runs the universe is still on His throne. He is not shaking or worried. He is the same yesterday, today, and forever.

God Is Greater Than Our Ideas

As you learn these things, you might feel like your head is spinning. That is a good sign! If we could fit God inside our small minds, He wouldn't be much of a God. He is supposed to be bigger than us.

We study these truths so we can worship Him for who He really is. We don't want to worship a "god" we made up in our own heads. We want to know the real God—the one who is all-knowing, all-present, all-powerful, and perfectly loving.

Reflect and Talk

1. Which of the "Omni" words (Omniscience, Omnipresent, Omnipotent) gives you the most comfort right now? Why?

2. Why is it important that God never changes? How would your life feel if God changed His mind about His promises?

3. Since God is holy and pure, how should that change the way we think about the "little" sins we often ignore?

CHAPTER 4

THREE PERSONS, ONE GOD (THE TRINITY)

Most math is easy. One plus one plus one equals three. But when we look at who God is, we find a different kind of math. One plus one plus one equals one. This is the doctrine of the Trinity.

The word "Trinity" is not actually in the Bible. Christians created the word to describe a truth that appears on almost every page of Scripture. It is the belief that there is one God who exists eternally in three Persons: the Father, the Son, and the Holy Spirit.

If this feels hard to grasp, you are in good company. We are trying to describe a Creator who is far beyond our logic. But even if we cannot fully explain it, we can look at what God has told us.

The Basic Idea

To get the best start, we need to distinguish between a "Being" and a "Person."

- **Being** is the "What."
- **Person** is the "Who."

You are one being and one person. God is different. He is one Being (the only true God) but He is three Persons. These three Persons are not three separate gods. They are not three different "modes" of God. They are distinct, yet they are the same God. They have always existed together in perfect love.

Where Is This in the Bible?

The Bible makes two things very clear from the start. First, there is only one God. Second, the Father is God, Jesus is God, and the Holy Spirit is God.

1. The Old Testament Hints

Even in the first chapter of the Bible, we see hints. In Genesis 1:26, God says, "Let **us** make man in **our** image." Who is the "us"? God is talking within Himself. We see the Spirit of God hovering over the waters in the beginning. We see a God who is one, but also a plural "us."

2. The Baptism of Jesus

One of the clearest pictures of the Trinity happens when Jesus gets baptized.

- **The Son** (Jesus) is standing in the water.
- **The Holy Spirit** comes down like a dove.
- **The Father** speaks from heaven, saying, "This is my beloved Son."

All three Persons are present and active at the same time. They are not one person changing costumes. They are three distinct Persons acting together.

3. The Great Commission

Before Jesus went back to heaven, He told His followers to baptize new believers "in the **name** of the Father and of the Son and of the Holy Spirit" (Matthew 28:19). Notice He said "name" (singular), not "names" (plural). One name, three Persons.

Avoid the Common Mistakes

People often try to use analogies to explain the Trinity. While they try to help, most of them actually teach something wrong about God.

- **The Water Analogy:** Some say God is like water. It can be ice, liquid, or steam. This is an error called "Modalism." Water cannot be all three at the same time in the same way. But the Father, Son, and Spirit are always distinct.
- **The Egg Analogy:** Some say God is like an egg. It has a shell, a white, and a yolk. This is an error called "Partialism." It suggests that the Father is only one-third of God. In reality, each Person is fully God.
- **The Three-Leaf Clover:** This also suggests that each Person is just a piece of God.

It is better to admit that God is a mystery than to use a bad example that makes Him smaller than He is. God is unique. Nothing else in the universe is like Him.

Different Roles, Same Purpose

While the Father, Son, and Spirit are all equal in power and glory, they often take on different roles in our lives.

- **The Father** is the Planner. He is the one who chose to create the world. He sent the Son to save us. He is the source of all things.

- **The Son** (Jesus) is the Redeemer. He is the one who became a human. He lived the perfect life we could not live. He died on the cross and rose again. He is the one who makes us right with God.

- **The Holy Spirit** is the Helper. He is the one who lives inside believers. He gives us the strength to follow Jesus. He helps us pray and helps us grasp the truth of the Bible.

Think of a song with three-part harmony. It is one song, but each voice has a different part. When they sing together, it creates a beauty that one voice could not make alone.

> "May the grace of the Lord Jesus Christ, and the love of God, and the fellowship of the Holy Spirit be with you all." - *2 Corinthians 13:14*

Why This Matters to You

You might ask, "Does it really matter if God is three or one?" It matters for one very big reason: **Love.**

If God were only one Person, He could not have been "love" before He created the world. Who would He have loved? He would have been lonely. He would have needed to create us just to have someone to love.

But because God is a Trinity, He has always been in a relationship. The Father has loved the Son and the Spirit for all eternity. God does not *need* us. He is already perfectly happy and full of love within Himself.

This means He created you not because He was lonely, but because He wanted to share His love with you.

- **You are invited into a family.** When you follow Jesus, you are brought into the relationship that the Father, Son, and Spirit have enjoyed forever.
- **You have a model for community.** We were made to live with others because we were made by a God who lives in community.
- **Your salvation is secure.** Your rescue was planned by the Father, finished by the Son, and is kept safe by the Spirit.

Knowing the Trinity helps you see that God is not a cold, lonely force. He is a living, loving community. When you pray, you speak to the Father, through the Son, by the help of the Spirit. You are never alone.

Reflect and Talk

1. Why is it actually a good thing that we cannot fully explain the Trinity with our own logic?

2. How does the idea of God being a "community of Persons" change the way you think about your own friendships?

3. Look at the baptism of Jesus in Matthew 3:13–17. How do you see the three Persons working together in that moment?

CHAPTER 5

CREATOR OF ALL THINGS

Think about the last thing you made. Maybe it was a sketch in a notebook, a *level* in a video game, or a batch of cookies. To make those things, you needed materials. You needed paper and a pencil. You needed code and a computer. You needed flour, sugar, and an oven. Humans are great at "making" things, but we always start with something that already exists.

God is different. When God created the universe, He did not have a toolbox. He did not have a pile of star-dust or a set of blueprints. He started with nothing. In this chapter, we look at how God brought everything into existence and why that changes how you look at the world around you.

Everything from Nothing

The very first verse of the Bible says: *"In the beginning God created the heavens and the earth"* (Genesis 1:1). This tells us that before the universe began, there was only God. There was no space, no time, and no matter.

Theologians use a Latin phrase for this: *creatio ex nihilo*. It simply means "creation out of nothing."

How did He do it? He spoke. He did not have to sweat or struggle. He said, "Let there be light," and light existed. This shows us the sheer power of God's word. When God speaks, reality changes. The stars, the planets, the deep oceans, and the microscopic cells in your body all exist because God willed them to be. They are not accidents. They are the result of a deliberate, intelligent choice by a powerful Creator.

The Universe Is a Mirror

God did not just make a "blank" universe. He filled it with variety, color, and order. Every part of creation tells us something about the Person who made it.

- **His Power:** Think about the sun. It is a massive ball of fire 93 million miles away. It is so powerful that it keeps our whole solar system in place. Yet, it is just one of billions of stars. The God who made the sun is much more powerful than the sun itself.

- **His Wisdom:** Look at the way an ecosystem works. Plants make oxygen. Animals breathe it. The water cycle moves rain from the sea to the fields. Everything is timed perfectly. This shows that God is a Master Designer.

- **His Beauty:** Why are there so many shades of blue in the ocean? Why do sunsets turn purple and orange? God did not have to make the world beautiful for it to work, but He did. This tells us He is a God who loves beauty.

When you look at nature, you are looking at God's artwork. It is meant to point you back to Him.

It Was "Very Good"

In Genesis 1, God stops after each day of work to look at what He made. He says, "It is good." At the very end, He looks at everything together and says it is "very good."

This is important because some people think the physical world is bad or "lesser" than spiritual things. They think that only "church stuff" matters to God. But that is not true. God made the physical world. He made your body. He made the food you eat and the air you breathe.

Because God made these things, they have value.

- Science is a way of studying God's handiwork.
- Art is a way of reflecting God's creativity.
- Athletics is a way of using the bodies God designed.

The world is broken now because of sin (which we will talk about later), but the "stuff" of the world is still fundamentally good because it belongs to God.

It is easy to get confused about the relationship between God and His world. There are two main mistakes people make:

1. **Thinking God is the world (Pantheism):** Some people believe that God *is* the trees, the stars, and the people. They think the universe is just part of God. The Bible says no. God is distinct from what He made. A painter is not the same thing as the painting.

2. **Thinking God is far away (Deism):** Some believe God made the world like a clock, wound it up, and then walked away. They think He doesn't care what happens now. The Bible says no to this, too. God is "sustaining all things by his powerful word" (Hebrews 1:3). If God stopped thinking about the universe for one second, it would cease to exist.

God is above the world (transcendent) but He is also very close to the world (immanent). He is the King of the universe, but He also counts the hairs on your head.

> "For in him all things were created: things in heaven and on earth, visible and invisible, whether thrones or powers or rulers or authorities; all things have been created through him and for him." - *Colossians 1:16*

The "Why" Behind the "What"

Why did God bother to make all of this? He didn't need us. As we learned in the chapter on the Trinity, God was already perfectly happy and loved within Himself.

God created the world for His **glory**.

Think of a "glory" like a great light or a reputation. God wanted to put His character on display. He wanted to share His goodness and His joy with others. The universe is like a giant stage where God's story is being told. Every mountain, every whale, and every human being exists to show how great God is.

When we live for our own glory, we feel empty. We were not made to be the center of the story. When we live for God's glory, we find our true purpose. We are like small mirrors reflecting a massive Sun.

Understanding God as Creator changes your perspective on three things:

1. Your Value You are not a cosmic accident. You are not just a collection of chemicals that happened to stick together. You were planned. God thought of you before the world began. He designed your DNA. He gave you your specific talents and your personality. You have value because the Creator of the universe made you on purpose.

2. Your Stewardship If God made the world, it belongs to Him. We are just "renters" or "managers." This means we should take care of the earth. We should treat animals with kindness. We should use the environment wisely. We don't protect nature because we worship nature; we protect nature because we love the One who made it.

3. Your Worship When you see something amazing, like a huge mountain range or a photo from a space telescope, your first instinct is to say, "Wow!" That "wow" is actually the beginning of worship. Don't stop at being amazed by the thing. Be amazed by the God who made the thing. The universe is a finger pointing toward God. Don't just stare at the finger; look where it is pointing.

Reflect and Talk

1. If God made everything "out of nothing," what does that tell you about His ability to handle the problems in your life?

2. What is your favorite part of creation (a specific animal, a type of weather, a place)? What does that specific thing tell you about God's personality?

3. How does knowing you were "made on purpose" change how you feel about yourself on a bad day?

PART THREE

THE PROBLEM

CHAPTER 6

BUILT IN HIS IMAGE

If you go to a zoo, you might spend time watching the chimpanzees. They are smart. They use tools to get food. They play with each other. They even seem to have feelings. You might look at them and think, *They are almost like us.* But there is a massive gap between the smartest animal and the simplest human being.

You can write a poem. You can pray. You can feel guilt when you do something wrong. You can plan for a future that is decades away. Where do these abilities come from? The Bible gives a specific answer. It says that humans are the crown of creation. We are the only part of the world that God made "in His image."

What Is the Image of God?

In Genesis 1:26, God says, "Then God said, "Let us make mankind in our image, in our likeness, so that they may rule over the fish in the sea and the birds in the sky, over the livestock and all the wild animals, and over all the creatures that move along the ground." Theologians call this the **Imago Dei**.

This does not mean God has a physical body and we look like Him. As we learned, God is spirit. Being made in His image means we reflect His character. We are like small mirrors designed to show what God is like to the rest of the world.

There are four main ways we reflect the image of God:

1. We Can Think (Rationality)

God has a mind. He plans and designs. He gave us the ability to think, reason, and solve problems. We can use logic. We can learn languages and tell stories. No other creature on earth can study the stars or write a symphony. We have an intellect because God has an intellect.

2. We Can Choose (Morality)

Animals act on instinct. A lion does not feel "guilty" for hunting a zebra. It is just doing what lions do. But you have a conscience. You have a sense of right and wrong. You know that some things are fair and others are cruel. This moral sense comes from God, who is perfectly holy and just.

3. We Can Love (Relationships)

God is a Trinity. He has lived in a relationship of love forever. Because He made us in His image, we are social beings. We crave friendship. We want to be known and loved. We find our greatest joy when we are in a healthy relationship with God and with other people.

4. We Can Create (Creativity)

God is the Great Creator. He made the world out of nothing. We cannot make things out of nothing, but we love to take what is already here and turn it into something new. Whether you are coding a website, painting a picture, or building a shelf, you are using the creative spark God put inside you.

Our Job Description

God did not just make us to look like Him. He gave us a job to do: "God blessed them and said to them, "Be fruitful and increase in number; fill the earth and subdue it. Rule over the fish in the sea and the birds in the sky and over every living creature that moves on the ground." (Genesis 1:28).

This is not a license to be a bully or to ruin the planet. It means we are God's "vice-regents." Think of a king who goes on a trip and leaves his son in charge of the palace. The son does not own the palace, but he is responsible for making sure everything runs well.

We are called to manage the world on God's behalf. We are meant to bring order out of chaos. We are meant to help things grow and flourish. When we take care of the environment, help the poor, or invent things that make life better, we are doing the job God gave us.

The Basis of Human Dignity

This truth is the most important foundation for how we treat people. Why is it wrong to bully someone? Why is it wrong to ignore someone who is suffering? Why do we care about the elderly or people with disabilities?

In a world without God, people often decide value based on what you can *do*. If you are smart, rich, or athletic, you have value. If you are weak or "unproductive," you don't.

But the Bible says your value is not based on what you do. It is based on who you *are*. Every single human being, no matter their race, their age, or their health, is a bearer of the image of God.

- The person who disagrees with you is an image-bearer.
- The person on the other side of the world is an image-bearer.
- The person you find difficult to like is an image-bearer.

If you insult a person, you are insulting the God who made them. If you show kindness to a person, you are honoring the Image of God.

> "With the tongue we praise our Lord and Father, and with it we curse human beings, who have been made in God's likeness. Out of the same mouth come praise and cursing. My brothers and sisters, this should not be." - *James 3:9–10*

A Broken Mirror

We have to be honest. While we are made in God's image, we don't always act like it. If you drop a mirror on the floor, it shatters. It is still a mirror. It still reflects light. But the reflection is now distorted and cracked.

That is what happened to us. Because of sin (which we will study in the next chapter), the image of God in us is broken. We still have the ability to think, love, and create, but we often use those gifts for the wrong reasons. We use our minds to lie. We use our creativity to hurt others.

The good news of the Bible is that God is in the business of fixing the mirror. When we follow Jesus, God begins to restore His image in us. He starts to make us look like Him again.

1. You Have Instant Value You live in a world that constantly tells you that you aren't enough. You aren't thin enough, smart enough, or popular enough. The doctrine of the *Imago Dei* shuts those lies down. You have dignity because God stamped His image on your soul. You don't have to earn your worth. You were born with it.

2. You Have a Purpose You are not here to just exist and then die. You are here to represent God. Every day is a chance to show the world what God is like through your words and your actions. You are an ambassador for the King of the universe.

3. You Have a Reason to Respect Others This changes how you walk down the hallways at school. It changes how you talk to your parents. Every person you see is a "masterpiece" of God's creation. Even the people who are hard to love deserve your respect because of whose image they carry.

Reflect and Talk

1. Which of the four ways we reflect God (thinking, choosing, loving, creating) do you feel is strongest in your life right now?

2. How would our schools or social media change if every teen treated others as "image-bearers" of God?

3. Knowing that you were made to "reflect" God, what is one thing about His character you want people to see when they look at your life?

CHAPTER 7

WHAT WENT WRONG?

If you spend five minutes watching the news or scrolling through social media, you see a clear pattern. The world is a mess. We see wars, poverty, and people treating each other with cruelty. Even in your own life, you feel it. You feel the sting of a friend's lie. You feel the sadness of losing a grandparent. You feel the frustration of your own mistakes.

In the last chapter, we saw that God made everything "very good." So, what happened? Why is the world so full of pain? The Bible does not shy away from this question. It tells us that a great disaster occurred early in human history. This disaster changed everything. We call it "The Fall."

The Choice in the Garden

God placed the first two humans, Adam and Eve, in a perfect garden. They had everything they needed. They had a perfect relationship with God and with each other. But God did not want them to be robots. Love is only real if it is a choice.

To give them a choice, God gave them one rule. They could eat from any tree in the garden except for one: the Tree of the Knowledge of Good and Evil. God warned them that if they ate from it, they would die.

> Then came the serpent: "Now the serpent was more crafty than any of the wild animals the Lord God had made. He said to the woman, "Did God really say, 'You must not eat from any tree in the garden'?"(*Genesis 3:1*).

He convinced them that God was holding out on them. He told them that if they ate the fruit, they would be like God.

Adam and Eve chose to trust the serpent instead of their Creator. They took the fruit and ate. In that moment, the "very good" world was shattered.

What Is Sin?

We often think of sin as a list of "bad things" like lying or stealing. While those are sins, the root of sin is much deeper.

The word "sin" in the Bible often comes from an archery term that means **"to miss the mark."** Imagine an archer aiming at a bullseye. If the arrow lands anywhere else, he missed the mark. God is the bullseye. He is the standard of perfection. Anything we do, think, or say that falls short of His perfect character is sin.

At its heart, sin is **rebellion**. It is telling God, "I know better than You. I want to be the boss of my own life. I want to set my own rules." It is a rejection of God's authority and a lack of trust in His goodness.

The Four Broken Relationships

When Adam and Eve sinned, the consequences were immediate. Sin acted like a spiritual earthquake that cracked the foundation of every relationship.

1. Our Relationship with God

Before the Fall, Adam and Eve talked with God face-to-face. After they sinned, they felt shame for the first time. They tried to hide from God among the trees. Sin creates a wall between us and a holy God. Because God is life, turning away from Him leads to death.

2. Our Relationship with Ourselves

Sin brought shame and fear. We no longer feel "at home" in our own skin. We struggle with guilt, anxiety, and a sense that something is "off" inside of us. We are no longer the perfect reflection of God we were meant to be.

3. Our Relationship with Others

As soon as God asked Adam what happened, Adam blamed Eve. Eve blamed the Serpent. The perfect harmony between humans was gone. Now, we have conflict, jealousy, and war. Every argument you have with your parents or friends is a result of the Fall.

4. Our Relationship with Nature

Even the earth itself changed. God told Adam that the ground would now produce thorns and thistles. Work would be hard. Bodies would get sick and eventually die. The natural world is now "groaning" for everything to be made right again.

Theologians use a heavy term to describe our current state: **Total Depravity**.

This does not mean that every person is as bad as they could possibly be. It does not mean you never do anything kind or helpful. It means that sin has touched every single part of who you are.

Think of a glass of water. If you put one drop of black ink into the glass, the ink spreads. It touches every molecule of the water. You can no longer say the water is pure.

In the same way, sin has affected our minds, our emotions, our bodies, and our wills. We are born with a "sin nature." This is why a toddler does not have to be taught how to throw a tantrum or hit a sibling. We are born with a heart that naturally wanders away from God.

> "As it is written: "There is no one righteous, not even one; there is no one who understands; there is no one who seeks God. All have turned away, they have together become worthless; there is no one who does good, not even one."- *Romans 3:10-12*

If the story ended there, it would be the most depressing book ever written. But right in the middle of the mess, God gave a promise.

While God was explaining the consequences of sin to the serpent, He said something strange: "And I will put enmity between you and the woman, and between your offspring and hers; he will crush your head, and you will strike his heel." (Genesis 3:15).

This is the first "Gospel" message in the Bible. God promised that one day, a human descendant would come to crush the head of the Serpent. This Savior would be "bruised" in the process, but He would win the final victory. Even before Adam and Eve left the garden, God had a rescue plan in motion.

1. It Explains Reality Have you ever wondered why it is so hard to be "good"? Have you wondered why there is so much hate in the world? The doctrine of the Fall gives you the answer. You don't have to be confused by the darkness. You know why it is there.

2. It Keeps You Humble Knowing that you have a sin nature stops you from being "judgey" toward others. You realize that you have the same capacity for wrong as anyone else. You see that you cannot fix yourself. You are not just a "good person who makes mistakes." You are a person in need of a rescue.

3. It Points You to Your True Need If our main problem was a lack of information, we would just need better schools. If our main problem was poverty, we would just need more money. But if our main problem is sin, we need a Savior.

Understanding what went wrong is the only way to appreciate what God did to fix it. You have to know the bad news before the Good News makes any sense. You are a broken image-bearer, but you are still loved by the God who wants to put the pieces back together.

Reflect and Talk

1. When you look at the world today, where do you see the "thorns and thistles" of the Fall most clearly?

2. Why is it easier to blame someone else (like Adam did) than to admit our own part in a problem?

3. How does knowing that every person is "fallen" change the way you look at people who have hurt you?

PART FOUR

THE RESCUE

CHAPTER 8

WHO IS JESUS?

In the last chapter, we looked at the "Bad News." Humans broke the world through sin, and we cannot fix it ourselves. If the story ended there, it would be a tragedy. But the heart of the Bible is the "Good News" about a Person.

If you ask people on the street who Jesus is, you will get many answers. Some say He was a great moral teacher. Others say He was a social revolutionary or a prophet. But the Bible makes a claim that is much more shocking. It tells us that Jesus is the Son of God who became a man to save us. To understand theology, you must understand the person of Jesus Christ.

Fully God: The Word Was God

The Bible begins the story of Jesus long before He was born in a manger. The Apostle John tells us that "In the beginning was the Word, and the Word was with God, and the Word was God" (John 1:1). Jesus didn't start existing in Bethlehem. He has existed forever as the second Person of the Trinity.

There are three big reasons we know Jesus is fully God:

1. **He did what only God can do.** He calmed storms with a word, walked on water, and raised people from the dead. Most importantly, He forgave sins; something the religious leaders of His day rightly said only God has the authority to do.

2. **He claimed to be God.** Jesus said, "I and the Father are one" (John 10:30). He used the name "I AM" for Himself, which was the sacred name God gave to Moses.

3. **He accepted worship.** In the Bible, good men and angels always refuse worship. But Jesus allowed people to bow down and worship Him as Lord.

If Jesus is not God, He cannot save us. A mere man cannot pay for the sins of the whole world. Only the infinite God can pay an infinite debt.

Fully Man: The Word Became Flesh

The most amazing miracle in history is the **Incarnation**. This word means "taking on flesh." The God who created the stars became a tiny embryo in the womb of a teenage girl named Mary.

Jesus was not a "ghost" or a God pretending to be a human. He was a real man.

- **He grew tired.** He had to sit down and rest.
- **He got hungry and thirsty.** He asked people for water and food.
- **He felt emotions.** He felt deep joy, and He wept with sorrow when His friend died.
- **He was tempted.** He felt the pull of temptation, yet He never once gave in to sin.

Why did He have to be human? Because humans are the ones who sinned. To be our substitute, Jesus had to be one of us. He had to live the perfect human life that we failed to live.

Two Natures, One Person

Theologians use a fancy term for this: the **Hypostatic Union**. It simply means that Jesus is one Person with two natures. He is 100% God and 100% man at the same time.

Think of it this way:

- As God, He knows everything; as man, He grew in wisdom.
- As God, He sustains the universe; as man, He needed to sleep.

He didn't lose His "God-hood" when He became a man. He just added a human nature to His divine nature. He is the bridge between heaven and earth. Because He is both, He can take the hand of a holy God and the hand of a sinful human and bring them together.

The Three Offices of Jesus

In the Old Testament, God used three main types of leaders to help His people. Jesus came to be the perfect version of all three.

1. The Prophet

A prophet speaks God's words to the people. Jesus didn't just speak God's words; He *is* the Word. He told us the truth about God, life, and the future. When we listen to Jesus, we are hearing exactly what God wants to say to us.

2. The Priest

A priest represents the people before God and offers sacrifices for their sins. Jesus is our Great High Priest. He didn't offer a goat or a lamb; He offered Himself as the final sacrifice. Now, He stands in heaven praying for us and making sure we have access to the Father.

3. The King

A king rules and protects his people. Jesus is the King of kings. He has authority over every atom in the universe. One day, He will return to set up a kingdom where there is no more crying or pain. Right now, He wants to be the King of your heart.

> "The Son is the image of the invisible God, the firstborn over all creation." - *Colossians 1:15*

Why This Matters to You

1. God Understands You Because Jesus became a man, God knows what it feels like to be you. He knows what it's like to be tired, stressed, or lonely. He knows the pain of being betrayed by a friend. When you pray, you aren't talking to a distant computer; you are talking to a Savior who has walked in your shoes.

2. You Can See What God Is Like Do you want to know how God feels about people who are hurting? Look at Jesus. Do you want to know how God feels about hypocrisy and pride? Look at Jesus. He is the "visible image of the invisible God." If you know Jesus, you know the Father.

3. He Is the Only Way Because Jesus is the only God-man, He is the only one qualified to bridge the gap caused by sin. No other religious leader or philosophy can do what He did. He is the only one who lived a perfect life and the only one who could pay for our rebellion.

1. Why is it important that Jesus is *fully* God? What would happen to our faith if He were just a "really good man"?

2. Why is it important that Jesus is *fully* human? How does it make you feel to know that He experienced the same struggles you do?

3. If Jesus is the "King" of your life, what is one area where you need to let Him lead you this week?

CHAPTER 9

THE WORK OF THE CROSS

If you walk into a jewelry store at the mall, you will likely see a whole section dedicated to crosses. You can buy them in gold, silver, or covered in diamonds. You see them printed on t-shirts, tattooed on arms, and placed on top of church steeples. The cross has become the most recognized symbol of the Christian faith. It is so common that we often forget what it actually is.

In the ancient Roman world, the cross was not a piece of fashion. It was a tool of terror. It was an instrument of torture designed to kill a person as slowly and painfully as possible. It was reserved for the worst criminals, rebels, and slaves. For a Roman citizen, the very idea of crucifixion was so shameful that they would not even speak of it in polite society.

So, why do Christians cherish this symbol? Why do we sing songs about it? Why do we call the day Jesus died "Good Friday"? The answer is that the cross is the turning point of history. It is where the holy justice of God and the infinite love of God collided. To understand Christianity, you must understand what happened on that hill outside of Jerusalem. It was not just a martyrdom; it was a rescue mission.

The Cup of Wrath

To understand the cross, we have to go back to the Garden of Gethsemane. This happened the night before Jesus died. The Bible tells us that Jesus was in agonizing pain. He was so stressed that He sweat drops of blood. He prayed a very specific prayer: "Going a little farther, he fell with his face to the ground and prayed, "My Father, if it is possible, may this cup be taken from me. Yet not as I will, but as you will." (Matthew 26:39)

What was in the "cup"? Was Jesus afraid of the physical pain? Surely, He knew the nails would hurt. But many martyrs throughout history have died bravely, singing hymns while they were burned at the stake. Jesus was afraid of something far worse than physical death.

In the Old Testament, the "cup" is often a symbol of God's wrath. It represents the anger of a holy God against sin. Imagine a cup filled with every lie, every hateful thought, every act of selfishness, and every moment of pride. Now add the sins of every person who has ever lived. God, because He is good, hates this evil. Justice demands a penalty. That is what was in the cup. Jesus was about to drink that cup down to the dregs, experiencing the full weight of judgment for us.

The Great Exchange

Theologians call what happened on the cross **Penal Substitutionary Atonement**. That is a mouthful, but the concept is simple and beautiful.

- **Penal:** It involves a legal penalty or punishment.
- **Substitutionary:** Jesus took our place.
- **Atonement:** The broken relationship is fixed; we are made "at one" with God.

Think of it as a "Great Exchange." Imagine you are standing in a courtroom. You have a stack of treason accusations against the King. You are guilty. Suddenly, the King's Son walks in. He has a perfect record. He looks at the judge and says, "I will take his punishment. Put his crimes on my record, and give him my freedom."

On the cross, God treated Jesus as if He had lived your life. He was punished for your mistakes. In exchange, God treats you as if you had lived Jesus' life. You get His perfect score. This is why the cross is the only way to be saved. We cannot pay our own debt. Only Jesus could pay it.

Four Words That Change Everything

When we talk about the work of the cross, the Bible uses four key words to describe what Jesus accomplished. Each word gives us a different angle on the diamond of salvation.

1. **Propitiation (Satisfying the Anger)** God is holy. His holiness burns against sin like fire burns up paper. Jesus offered Himself as the sacrifice that absorbed that fire. Because of the cross, God's wrath toward believers is exhausted. There is none left for you. When God looks at you now, He is not angry; He is pleased.

2. **Redemption (Buying Freedom)** This word comes from the ancient slave markets. If a person was a slave, someone could pay a "ransom" to buy their freedom. The Bible says we were slaves to sin. Jesus paid the ransom price. The cost was not silver or gold; it was His own blood. You belong to God now because He bought you back.

3. **Justification (Legal Standing)** This is a legal term. It is the opposite of condemnation. It doesn't just mean "innocent", it means "righteous." Because Jesus gave you His record, you are legally righteous in God's eyes. It is "just as if" you never sinned.

4. **Reconciliation (Restoring Friendship)** Sin did not just break a law; it broke a relationship. It made us enemies of God. The cross is the peace treaty. It removed the barrier of sin that stood between us and God. Now, we are not just citizens; we are friends and family.

Toward the end of His time on the cross, Jesus shouted one final word in Greek: *Tetelestai.* We translate this as "It is finished." In those days, this word was often written on tax receipts. It meant "Paid in Full."

Jesus was not admitting defeat. He was shouting a victory cry. He was declaring that the work of salvation was complete. The debt of sin was zeroed out. At that moment, the thick curtain in the Temple that separated people from God's presence tore in two from top to bottom. God tore it. He was showing the world that the barrier was gone. Because the debt was paid, we can now come into the presence of a holy God without fear.

> *"For Christ also suffered once for sins, the righteous for the unrighteous, to bring you to God. He was put to death in the body but made alive in the Spirit." - 1 Peter 3:18*

1. **You Do Not Have to Pay** Many of us live with a low-level sense of guilt. We feel like we need to "make up" for our mistakes. The cross tells us that the debt is already paid. You cannot add to His payment. You are free to obey God out of love and gratitude, not out of fear or guilt.

2. **You Are Defined by Love** How do you know someone loves you? You look at what they are willing to sacrifice for you. God did not wait for you to get your act together; He died for you while you were still a sinner. When you feel worthless, look at the cross. It is God's proof of how much He wants you.

3. **You Have a Safe Anchor** Life is shaky, and feelings change. But the work of the cross is a historical fact. Your standing with God does not depend on how good you feel today; it depends on what Jesus did 2,000 years ago. That is a rock you can build your life on.

Reflect and Talk

1. Why is it important to understand that the "cup" Jesus drank was not just physical death, but spiritual judgment?

2. If someone asked you, "How can one man pay for the sins of the whole world?", how would you use the concept of the "Great Exchange" to explain it?

3. Which of the four words (Propitiation, Redemption, Justification, Reconciliation) makes you feel the most grateful today? Why?

CHAPTER 10

OUR ADVOCATE (THE HOLY SPIRIT)

If you have ever tried to follow Jesus on your own strength, you probably realized pretty quickly that it is hard. You might start the day with great intentions, but by lunchtime, you've lost your temper, or you've let a selfish thought take over. It can feel like trying to drive a car with no gasoline, you can steer it and polish it, but it isn't going anywhere.

The good news is that God never intended for you to live the Christian life alone. Before Jesus went to the cross, He told His disciples something shocking: He said: "But very truly I tell you, it is for your good that I am going away. Unless I go away, the Advocate will not come to you; but if I go, I will send him to you." (John 16:7). That is the Holy Spirit. He is not a "vibe," a "feeling," or a ghostly mist; He is the third Person of the Trinity, and He is the power source for your life.

Who Is the Holy Spirit?

As we learned in the chapter on the Trinity, the Holy Spirit is fully God. He isn't a "junior partner" in the Godhead, nor is He "lesser" than the Father or the Son. He has a mind, emotions, and a will. The Bible tells us: "And do not grieve the Holy Spirit of God, with whom you were sealed for the day of redemption." (Ephesians 4:30)

In the Old Testament, the Holy Spirit would "come upon" specific people for specific tasks, like giving King Solomon wisdom or giving an artist the skill to build the Tabernacle. But after Jesus rose from the dead and went to heaven, something radical happened. On the day of Pentecost, the Holy Spirit was poured out on *all* believers. Now, if you belong to Jesus, the Holy Spirit doesn't just visit you; He lives inside you.

The Spotlight: The Spirit's Main Mission

One of the most important things to understand about the Holy Spirit is that He is humble. He doesn't seek the limelight. Theologians often describe His work as a "floodlight ministry." If you walk past a beautiful monument at night, you don't stare at the floodlights on the ground; you look at the monument they are shining on.

The Holy Spirit's primary mission is to point to Jesus. He helps you understand the Bible, reminds you of God's promises, and makes the person of Jesus feel "real" to you. When you suddenly feel a deep sense of love for God or a clear understanding of a Bible verse, that isn't just your brain working, that is the Holy Spirit shining His spotlight on the truth.

The Work of the Spirit: Conviction and New Life

The Holy Spirit's work starts before you even become a Christian. He is the one who "opens your eyes." Without His help, the things of God seem like foolishness to us.

1. Regeneration (New Birth)

The Bible says that because of sin, our spirits were "dead." We couldn't fix ourselves. The Holy Spirit is the one who performs "spiritual CPR." He breathes life into our souls. This is what Jesus meant by being "born again." The Spirit changes our hearts of stone into hearts of flesh that actually want to love God.

2. Conviction

Have you ever done something wrong and felt a sudden "tug" or "heavy weight" in your heart? That isn't just a bad feeling; it is the Holy Spirit. He "convicts" us of sin. He isn't doing this to shame us or make us feel like garbage. He does it because He loves us. He shows us the truth about our sin so that we will turn back to the Father for forgiveness. He is like a doctor pointing out a sickness so that He can provide the cure.

The Internal Power Source: Sanctification

Once the Holy Spirit moves in, He begins a lifelong project called **Sanctification**. This is the process of making you more like Jesus. It is a partnership: you choose to obey, but the Spirit provides the power to actually do it.

The Fruit of the Spirit

You cannot "force" yourself to be a truly joyful or patient person any more than an apple tree can "force" itself to grow apples. Growth comes from the "sap" inside. When you stay connected to God, the Holy Spirit produces "fruit" in your life: love, joy, peace, patience, kindness, goodness, faithfulness, gentleness, and self-control (Galatians 5:22-23). These aren't just personality traits; they are the character of Jesus being grown inside of you.

Power Over Temptation

On your own, you might give in to temptation every time. But the Bible says: "And if the Spirit of him who raised Jesus from the dead is living in you, he who raised Christ from the dead will also give life to your mortal bodies because of his Spirit who lives in you." (Romans 8:11) This means you have access to supernatural strength. When you feel a temptation to lie or to be greedy, you can ask the Holy Spirit for help. He provides the "way of escape" and the strength to say "no."

Spiritual Gifts: Tools for the Family

The Holy Spirit doesn't just give you "fruit" (character); He also gives you "gifts" (abilities). Every single believer is given at least one spiritual gift. These aren't for showing off; they are "tools" given to help the Church.

- **Communication Gifts:** Like teaching, encouragement, or sharing the Gospel.
- **Service Gifts:** Like helping others, being generous, or leadership.
- **Support Gifts:** Like wisdom, faith, or showing mercy to those who are hurting.

The Spirit decides who gets which gift. You don't have to be jealous of someone else's gift, and you shouldn't feel useless because you don't have theirs. You are like a piece of a puzzle; the Holy Spirit has given you exactly what you need to help the "Big Picture" of God's plan.

The Seal and the Guarantee

In the ancient world, when a king sent a letter, he would melt wax on the envelope and press his signet ring into it. This was a "seal." It proved who owned the letter and guaranteed it wouldn't be messed with.

The Bible says the Holy Spirit is God's "seal" on your life (Ephesians 1:13-14). He is also called a "deposit" or a "guarantee." When the Holy Spirit moves into your heart, He is God's way of saying, "This person belongs to Me, and I am going to finish the work I started." He is the down payment on the eternal life you will one day have in heaven.

"The Spirit himself testifies with our spirit that we are God's children." - *Romans 8:16*

Walking by the Spirit

How do we actually interact with the Holy Spirit? The Bible uses the phrase "Walk by the Spirit."

Walking is a slow, steady, step-by-step process. It means staying in constant communication with Him.

- **Listening:** We listen to the Spirit by reading the Bible, because the Spirit is the one who inspired the authors to write it. He will never tell you to do something that contradicts the Bible.

- **Surrendering:** It means saying, "Not my will, but Yours." When you feel that nudge to apologize to a friend, or to spend time praying instead of scrolling on your phone, that is an invitation to walk with Him.

- **Depending:** It means admitting, "Holy Spirit, I can't do this today without You. Please give me Your patience and Your love."

Why This Matters to You

1. You are Never Truly Alone One of the titles Jesus gave the Holy Spirit is "The Comforter." When you feel lonely, misunderstood, or abandoned, remember that God Himself lives within you. He is closer to you than your own breath. You have a constant Friend who knows your thoughts and feels your pain.

2. You Don't Have to Be "Perfect" Today The Christian life isn't about you trying harder to be good so that God will love you. It's about you being loved by God and letting the Holy Spirit change you from the inside out. You can stop stressing about your performance and start trusting His power.

3. You Have a Purpose and the Power to Fulfill It Do you feel like you have nothing to offer? The Holy Spirit disagrees. He has placed specific gifts in you that the world needs. Because He is in you, you can do things you never thought possible—like forgiving someone who deeply hurt you, or finding peace in the middle of a massive life storm.

Reflect and Talk

1. Why is it more comforting to know the Holy Spirit is a *Person* you can have a relationship with, rather than just an "energy" or a "power source"?

2. Look at the list of the Fruit of the Spirit in Galatians 5:22-23. Which of those do you see the Holy Spirit growing in you right now? Which one do you feel you need the most help with this week?

3. How does the idea of the Holy Spirit being a "seal" or a "guarantee" change how you feel about your security in God?

PART FIVE

THE GIFT

CHAPTER 11

SAVED BY GRACE ALONE

Imagine you are deep underwater, far below the surface where the light can't reach. Your lungs are burning, you are out of oxygen, and you are completely unable to swim back up on your own. You don't need a "how-to" manual on swimming. You don't need someone to give you a pep talk about trying harder. You need someone to dive in, grab you, and pull you to the surface. You need a rescue.

This is the heart of the doctrine of **Grace**. In the previous chapters, we looked at how great God is and how broken we are. Now we ask the most important question: *How does a person get right with God?* The answer isn't "try harder" or "be better." The answer is a single word: Grace.

Grace vs. Mercy vs. Justice

To understand grace, we have to distinguish it from two other words we often use in church.

- **Justice** is getting what you *do* deserve. (If you break the law and get a fine, that's justice.)

- **Mercy** is *not* getting what you *do* deserve. (If you break the law but the judge lets you off without the fine, that's mercy.)

- **Grace** is getting what you *do not* deserve. (If the judge lets you off the fine and then gives you $1,000 to start over, that's grace.)

In the Gospel, God gives us all three. He satisfies **Justice** by punishing Jesus for our sins. He shows **Mercy** by not punishing us. And He pours out **Grace** by giving us eternal life and adopting us into His family.

The "Un-Earnable" Gift

The most common mistake people make about Christianity is thinking that it is a "ladder" we climb to get to God. We think if we pray enough, read our Bibles enough, and stay out of trouble, God will finally accept us.

But the Bible says the exact opposite: "David says the same thing when he speaks of the blessedness of the one to whom God credits righteousness apart from works:" (Romans 4:6). This means there is absolutely nothing you can do to make God love you more, and nothing you have done that makes Him love you less.

If you could earn your way into heaven, then Jesus wouldn't have needed to die. If you could be "good enough," then salvation would be a paycheck you earned, not a gift you received. But because salvation is a gift, no one can brag about it.

Faith: The Hand that Receives

If grace is the gift, **Faith** is the hand that reaches out to take it.

Faith is often misunderstood. It isn't just "believing that God exists", even the demons believe that! True faith is **trust**. It is like sitting down in a chair. You don't just "believe" the chair will hold you; you actually put your weight on it.

We are saved when we stop putting our weight on our own "goodness" and put all our weight on what Jesus did on the cross. We stop saying "I am a good person" and start saying "Jesus is a great Savior."

The Five "Solas"

During a time in history called the Reformation, theologians came up with five Latin phrases (the "Solas") to protect the true meaning of grace. They serve as guardrails to keep us from falling into the trap of thinking we save ourselves.

1. **Sola Gratia (Grace Alone):** We are saved only by God's unmerited favor.

2. **Sola Fide (Faith Alone):** We receive this salvation only through trust, not by doing chores for God.

3. **Solus Christus (Christ Alone):** Jesus is the only bridge between us and the Father.

4. **Sola Scriptura (Scripture Alone):** The Bible is our only final authority for how to be saved.

5. **Soli Deo Gloria (Glory to God Alone):** Since God did all the work, He gets 100% of the credit.

   "For it is by grace you have been saved, through faith—and this is not from yourselves, it is the gift of God— not by works, so that no one can boast." - *Ephesians 2:8-9*

Grace is Not a License to Sin

Whenever you talk about "Grace Alone," someone always asks: "If I'm saved by grace and not by being good, does that mean I can just go out and sin all I want?"

The Apostle Paul answered: "By no means! We are those who have died to sin; how can we live in it any longer?" (Romans 6:2)

Think of it this way: If someone jumped into a freezing river and saved you from drowning at the cost of their own health, you wouldn't say, "Great! Now I'm going to go throw rocks at their house!" You would love them. You would want to do anything for them because you are so grateful.

Works are the *result* of salvation, not the *cause* of it. We don't do good things *to get* saved; we do good things because we *are* saved. Obedience is our "thank you" note to God.

Why This Matters to You

1. You Can Stop Performing Many teens feel a massive amount of pressure to be perfect, to have the best grades, the best body, or the best social media feed. Grace is the only place in the world where the pressure is off. You don't have to perform for God. You are already loved, accepted, and "righteous" in His eyes because of Jesus.

2. You Can Be Honest About Your Mess If you believe you are saved by being "good," you will always try to hide your mistakes. But if you are saved by grace, you can be honest. You can admit when you're struggling, because you know your standing with God isn't based on your perfection.

3. It Gives You a Heart for Others When you realize that you are a "beggar who found bread," you stop being judgmental toward other people. You realize that you aren't "better" than the person who doesn't know God; you're just a person who has been rescued by a very kind Savior.

Reflect and Talk

1. Why is it so hard for us to accept a "free gift"? Why do we always want to pay God back or prove we are worthy?

2. If you knew for 100% certainty that God's love for you would never change regardless of your performance, how would that change your stress levels this week?

3. How would you explain the difference between "Grace" and "Justice" to a friend who thinks they have to be "good enough" for God?

CHAPTER 12

REPENTANCE AND FAITH

Imagine you are driving down a long, straight highway at night. You're making great time, your favorite music is playing, and you feel completely in control. But then, you pass a road sign that glows under your headlights, and your heart sinks. You realize you've been driving North for the last hour when your destination is actually South.

What do you do? You don't just keep driving and hope the road eventually circles back. You don't just slow down to 20 mph to "sin less" while still heading the wrong way. To get where you need to be, you have to do something decisive: you have to stop the car, find a place to turn around, and head in the opposite direction.

In the Bible, this "U-turn" is the only proper response to the grace of God. It consists of two inseparable actions: **Repentance** and **Faith**. Theologians often call these the "two wings of an airplane" or "two sides of a coin." You cannot have one without the other. If you try to have faith without repentance, you're just adding Jesus to your old life. If you try to have repentance without faith, you're just trying to fix yourself without a Savior.

Repentance: More Than Just "I'm Sorry"

The word "repentance" often gets a bad reputation in our culture. We picture a sidewalk preacher shouting at people, or someone groveling in the dirt feeling miserable. But the biblical word for repentance is *metanoia*, which literally means "a change of mind." It's an intellectual, emotional, and volitional shift.

It is vital to distinguish between **Biblical Repentance** and **Worldly Regret**.

- **Regret** is being sorry you got caught. It's the feeling you get when you see the police lights in your rearview mirror. It is focused on *consequences*.

- **Repentance** is being sorry for the sin itself because it offends a holy God. It is focused on *character*.

True repentance involves three distinct layers:

1. Your Mind (Intellectual)

You stop making excuses for your behavior. You stop saying, "Well, I only lied because they started it," or "Everyone else is doing it." You agree with God that your sin is a rebellion against Him. You change your mind about who is the boss of your life.

2. Your Heart (Emotional)

The Bible calls this "godly sorrow." It's a deep grief over the fact that your sin has wounded the heart of the God who loves you and died for you. It's not a shame that makes you want to hide (like Adam and Eve in the bushes); it's a sorrow that makes you want to run *to* God for help.

3. Your Will (Volitional)

This is the action. You make a deliberate choice to turn away from the sin and turn toward God. It's like realizing you are holding a handful of poisonous snakes and dropping them immediately. You don't drop them because you're trying to earn a "Good Person" award; you drop them because you realize they are killing you and those around you.

Faith: The Anchor of the Soul

If repentance is the "turning away," then faith is the "turning to." As we touched on in the previous chapter, saving faith is far more than just "believing that God exists." The Bible tells us that even the demons believe God exists—and they tremble in fear (James 2:19).

Theologians describe three essential layers of faith that must work together:

- **Knowledge (*Notitia*):** You have to know the facts. You cannot have faith in a Jesus you've never heard of. You must know that He lived, died for sins, and rose again.

- **Agreement (*Assensus*):** You have to believe those facts are true. You agree that the Bible is accurate and that Jesus is indeed the Son of God.

- **Trust (*Fiducia*):** This is the "spark" of saving faith. This is when you personally rely on Jesus to save *you*.

Think of it like a chair. You can have the **knowledge** of how a chair is built. You can **agree** that the chair looks sturdy enough to hold a person. But you don't actually have "faith" in that chair until you put all your weight on it and lift your feet off the ground. Faith is "putting your weight" on the finished work of Jesus and trusting Him with your eternal destiny.

The Great Tug-of-War: The Coin with Two Sides

You cannot truly turn *to* God (Faith) without turning *away* from your old life (Repentance). Imagine you are holding a heavy bag of trash in your right hand. Someone stands before you and offers you a bar of solid gold. To reach out and take the gold, you *must* let go of the trash.

- **Repentance** is the act of letting go of the trash.
- **Faith** is the act of reaching out for the gold.

If you say you have "faith" but you refuse to let go of your secret sins or your desire to be your own god, your hands are too full to receive the gift Jesus is offering. Conversely, if you just "drop the trash" but never reach for Jesus, you're just a person standing in a mess with empty hands.

A Gift, Not a Work

One of the most mind-blowing things about theology is that even our ability to repent and believe is a gift from God.

If we are "dead in our sins" (as we learned in Chapter 7), a dead person cannot decide to wake up and have faith. God has to perform a miracle in our hearts first. He gives us the "eyes to see" how beautiful Jesus is and "ears to hear" the truth of the Gospel.

This keeps us humble. We can't get to heaven and brag, "I was smart enough to repent!" Instead, we say, "Thank You, God, for opening my eyes so I could see that I needed to turn around."

> "The time has come," he said. "The kingdom of God has come near. Repent and believe the good news!" - *Mark 1:15*

1. It's a Lifestyle, Not a One-Time Event Many people think repentance is something you do once to "get saved" and then you're done. But Martin Luther, a famous reformer, said that the entire life of a believer should be one of repentance. Following Jesus means that every day, we realize we've drifted off course, and every day, we turn back to Him. It's a lifestyle of honesty and "refreshing" your soul.

2. It Offers a Constant Fresh Start No matter how far you have driven in the wrong direction, a U-turn is always available. God's grace is bigger than your biggest failure. When you come to God in repentance, He doesn't say, "I told you so." He doesn't hold a grudge. He says, "Welcome home," and He wipes the slate clean.

3. It Removes the Pressure of "Strong Faith" Many teens worry, "Is my faith strong enough?" But here is the secret: It isn't the *strength* of your faith that saves you; it is the *Object* of your faith. Imagine two people crossing a frozen lake. One has "strong faith" and runs across confidently. The other has "weak faith" and crawls across trembling. If the ice is thick, both are safe. If the ice is thin, the confident person falls in just as fast as the trembling person. Our "ice" is Jesus. He is solid. Even if your faith feels small and shaky, if it is placed in a strong Savior, you are 100% secure.

Reflect and Talk

1. Why do you think people are often afraid of the word "Repentance"? How does the "U-turn" illustration make it feel more hopeful?

2. Looking at the three layers of faith (Knowledge, Agreement, Trust), which one do you think is the hardest for people your age to grasp?

3. Is there something in your life right now that feels like "trash" you need to let go of so you can reach out for the "gold" of God's grace?

CHAPTER 13

ADOPTED INTO THE FAMILY

Imagine for a moment that you are an orphan living on the streets of a massive, indifferent city. You have no last name, no bank account, and no one to look out for you. You are constantly worried about where your next meal will come from and where you will sleep. You are "invisible" to the world, just another person trying to survive.

Then, one day, the King of the country pulls up in his carriage. He doesn't just give you some spare change or a warm meal to keep you going for another night. He doesn't even just offer you a job in the palace kitchens. Instead, he brings you into his private study, signs a legal document with his royal seal, and says, "From now on, you are my child. You carry my name. My home is your home. Everything I have belongs to you."

In theology, we call this **Adoption**. While "Justification" is a legal term that says you are "not guilty" in the eyes of the law, Adoption is a relational term that says you are "home." It is the highest privilege the Gospel offers. It takes us from the courtroom of the Judge to the living room of the Father.

The Great Shift: From Enemy to Heir

To understand how massive this deal is, we have to remember where we started. Because of sin, the Bible doesn't describe us as "natural" children of God. In our culture, people often say, "We are all children of God." While it's true that we are all *creatures* made by God, the Bible is very specific that we are only *children* through Jesus. Before we met Christ, the Bible says: "Once you were alienated from God and were enemies in your minds because of your evil behavior." (Colossians 1:21). We weren't just "lost"; we were on the other side of a war.

When God saves us, He does something far beyond just pardoning our crimes. He brings us into the inner circle. He doesn't just let us into heaven as "guests" who have to stay in the lobby, or "servants" who work the grounds. He makes us family.

1. A New Status (The Name)

In the ancient world, adoption was a serious legal matter. When a child was adopted, their old debts were wiped out, and they received a new family name. They gained a new identity that could never be taken away. You are now a son or daughter of the Most High. This isn't just a title; it is the core of who you are.

2. A New Standing (The Access)

Think about the difference between a servant and a child. A servant has to knock, wait for permission, and enter the King's room with their head bowed, hoping they aren't interrupting. A child just walks in. A child can run into the Father's room at 3:00 AM because they had a bad dream, and the Father won't be angry, He'll open His arms. "In him and through faith in him we may approach God with freedom and confidence" (Ephesians 3:12).

3. A New Future (The Inheritance)

In ancient times, the "heir" was the one who inherited the father's entire estate. The Bible says we are "heirs of God and fellow heirs with Christ" (Romans 8:17). Stop and think about that for a second. Everything that belongs to Jesus, His joy, His victory, His closeness to the Father, His authority over the new creation, is shared with you. You aren't just getting a "ticket to heaven"; you are inheriting a Kingdom.

The Spirit of Adoption: The Inner Whisper

How do we know we are actually God's children? Is it just a legal theory written in a book somewhere? No. God gives us an internal "witness."

The Bible says that God has sent the "Spirit of adoption" into our hearts. This Spirit helps us cry out, *"Abba, Father!"* (Galatians 4:6). *Abba* is an Aramaic word that is very personal. It's a bit like a child saying "Papa" or "Dad" or "Dada." It's a term of deep, gut-level affection and trust.

The Holy Spirit works in us in two ways regarding our adoption:

First, He Assures Us. On your worst days, when you feel like a failure or when you feel like God must be disappointed in you, the Holy Spirit whispers to your heart, "You are still His. You are still a child." He reminds you that your position in the family isn't based on your performance but on the Father's promise.

Second, He Changes Us. The Spirit helps you start looking like your Father. Just like you might have your dad's eyes, your mom's laugh, or your grandfather's sense of humor, the Spirit helps you develop God's "family traits." You start to value what He values. You start to love people you used to ignore. You start to find joy in things that used to seem boring. This is the "family likeness" growing in you.

The Discipline of a Father: Proof of Love

Being adopted into God's family doesn't mean life is always easy or that you get everything you want. In fact, sometimes it feels like God is being "hard" on you. This can be confusing unless you understand the heart of a father.

Hebrews 12 tells us not to be discouraged when we face trials, because "the Lord disciplines the one he loves." Think about it this way: If you see a random kid at the park throwing a tantrum or being mean to others, you probably won't step in and correct him. Why? Because he's not your kid. You might think it's sad, but it's not your responsibility. But if your *own* child acts that way, you step in immediately. You might take away a toy, give them a "time out," or have a serious talk. You do this because you love them too much to let them grow up to be a jerk.

When God allows us to go through hard times or "corrects" our behavior through a guilty conscience or difficult circumstances, it is actually proof that we belong to Him. He isn't "punishing" us (Jesus already took our punishment on the cross); He is **training** us. He is pruning us so we can grow better. A good father cares more about his child's character than his child's comfort.

When you are adopted into a royal family, you don't just sit in the palace and eat grapes all day. You represent the family. You enter the "family business."

Our family business is the **Kingdom of God**. As children of the King, we are now ambassadors. We represent His interests on earth.

- **We Care What He Cares About:** We care about justice, mercy, and truth because our Father does. We stand up for the bullied and the broken because our Father is a "Father to the fatherless."

- **We Love the Other Kids:** Being adopted by God means you are also adopted into a massive, global family. Every other believer is your brother or sister. This means we treat other Christians with kindness and forgiveness, even when they are difficult, because we share the same Father.

- **We Invite Others In:** Our mission is to go back to the streets where we used to live and tell the other "orphans" that there is a King who wants to adopt them too. We aren't better than them; we're just kids who found a Father.

Why This Matters to You

1. Your Identity is Unshakeable In the ancient Roman world, an adoption was actually more permanent than a natural birth. Under Roman law, a father could disown a biological son, but a son who was *legally adopted* could never be disowned. God chose you. He knew exactly what He was getting when He brought you into the family. He knew your future mistakes and your hidden struggles, and He signed the papers anyway. You can rest in the fact that your place in the family is secure.

2. You Don't Have to Fear the Future If the King of the universe is your Dad, what do you really have to be afraid of? Stress about school, worries about what people think of you, and fears about the future all start to shrink when you realize the person in charge of the universe loves you as His own child. He has promised to provide for you and to never leave you.

3. You Have Total Access You don't need a priest, a "professional" Christian, or a perfect prayer life to talk to God. You are His child. You can go to Him with your smallest worries, like a test you're nervous about, and your biggest fears. He is never too busy for you, He never thinks your problems are "stupid," and He never grows tired of hearing your voice.

> "See what great love the Father has lavished on us, that we should be called children of God! And that is what we are! The reason the world does not know us is that it did not know him." - *1 John 3:1*

Reflect and Talk

1. What is the difference between thinking of God as a "Boss" and thinking of Him as a "Father"? How does that change the way you pray tonight?

2. If you truly believed that you were an "heir" of everything God owns, how would that change the way you feel when you feel "less than" or "not enough" at school?

3. How does knowing that God's discipline is a sign of *love* change how you look at the "rough patches" or "nos" you've received from Him lately?

PART SIX

THE NEW LIFE

CHAPTER 14

GROWING TO BE LIKE JESUS

Once you have been rescued by grace and adopted into God's family, a new question naturally pops up: *What now?* If you've ever watched a baby grow, you know it's a process. They don't walk the day they are born. They don't speak full sentences for a long time. But day by day, as they eat, sleep, and interact with their parents, they start to change. They start to look and act more like the family they belong to.

In theology, the word for this "growing up" process is **Sanctification**. While justification is God's work of declaring you "right" in a single moment, sanctification is God's work of making you "holy" over a lifetime. It is the journey of the "Old You" (the one ruled by sin) slowly being replaced by the "New You" (the one who looks like Jesus).

The Two Natures: A House Under Renovation

Imagine you buy a house that is falling apart. The roof leaks, the walls are covered in mold, and the foundation is cracked. When God saves you, He "buys" the house. But He doesn't just leave it that way. He moves in and starts a massive renovation project.

As a Christian, you often feel a "tug-of-war" inside you. The Apostle Paul described this in Romans 7. Part of you wants to love God and do what is right, but another part of you, which the Bible calls "the flesh", still wants to go back to your old ways.

- **The Flesh:** The leftover habits, desires, and selfishness of your old life.

- **The Spirit:** The new life God has placed in you that desires to please Him.

Sanctification is the process of "starving" the flesh and "feeding" the Spirit. It is not about being "perfect" today; it is about being more like Jesus today than you were yesterday.

Growth doesn't happen by accident, and it doesn't happen just by trying harder. An apple tree doesn't grow fruit by "gritting its teeth." It grows fruit by staying connected to the roots and getting sunlight and water. We grow by using the **Means of Grace**—the tools God has given us to stay connected to Him.

1. The Word of God (The Bible)

If you want to look like Jesus, you have to know what Jesus is like. The Bible is more than just a history book; it is "living and active." As you read it, the Holy Spirit uses it to rewire your brain, changing the way you think about yourself, others, and the world.

2. Prayer (The Connection)

Prayer is the "breath" of the Christian life. It is how we express our dependence on God. When we pray, we aren't just giving God a shopping list of things we want; we are aligning our hearts with His. We are asking Him for the strength to do what we can't do on our own.

3. Fellowship (The Community)

As we learned earlier, you cannot grow to be like Jesus in isolation. You need other Christians to encourage you, challenge you, and help you see the blind spots in your life. We are like "living stones" being built together.

4. Worship and Sacraments

Participating in the life of the church, singing together, taking communion, and witnessing baptisms, reminds us of the "Big Story" we are a part of. It pulls our focus off our own problems and puts it back on God's glory.

What does a "grown-up" Christian actually look like? It's not necessarily someone who has the most Bible verses memorized or someone who never makes a mistake. A person who is growing like Jesus is someone whose life is increasingly filled with the **Fruit of the Spirit** (Galatians 5:22-23).

Note that the Bible says "fruit" (singular), not "fruits." They are like a single cluster of grapes. God wants to grow *all* of them in you:

- **Love** that puts others first.
- **Joy** that doesn't depend on your circumstances.
- **Peace** that stays calm even when life is messy.
- **Patience** with people who are difficult.
- **Kindness and Goodness** in how you treat everyone.
- **Faithfulness** to your word and your God.
- **Gentleness and Self-Control** over your temper and your desires.

Progress, Not Perfection

One of the biggest traps for Christian teens is **Legalism**. This is the belief that God only likes you if you are performing well. When you fall back into an old sin or have a "bad day," legalism tells you that you've lost God's favor.

But sanctification is a marathon, not a sprint. There will be days when you stumble. There will be seasons where you feel like you're taking two steps forward and one step back.

The key is "Direction, not Perfection." Are you heading toward Jesus? When you fall, do you get back up and run toward Him, or do you stay in the dirt? God is the one doing the work in you, and He is very patient.

> "being confident of this, that he who began a good work in you will carry it on to completion until the day of Christ Jesus." - *Philippians 1:6*

Why This Matters to You

1. You Have a New Power Source You don't have to change yourself. You can't! The Holy Spirit is the one who produces the fruit. Your job is to "abide"—to stay close to Jesus. When you stop trying to "act" like a Christian and start "being" with Christ, the change happens naturally.

2. Your Life Gains Meaning Every situation you face, even the hard ones, is an opportunity to grow. A boring day at school is a chance to practice patience. A conflict with a friend is a chance to practice forgiveness. Nothing in your life is wasted because God is using everything to shape you into the image of His Son.

3. You Can Be Patient with Yourself You are a "work in progress." You don't have to have it all figured out yet. You can be honest about your struggles because you know that God isn't finished with you. He is a Master Artist, and He takes His time with His masterpieces.

Reflect and Talk

1. Why is it easier to try to "act" like a Christian (legalism) than to actually "grow" into one (sanctification)?

2. Looking at the Fruit of the Spirit, which one do you feel is most "in season" in your life right now? Which one feels like it's still just a tiny bud?

3. How does the promise in Philippians 1:6 (that God will *finish* the work) help you when you feel like you aren't changing fast enough?

CHAPTER 15

WHY WE NEED THE CHURCH

In the modern world, we love the idea of being "self-made." We have "DIY" projects, solo playlists, and the ability to order anything we want without ever talking to a human being. Many people bring this same "Lone Ranger" attitude to their faith. They say things like, "I love Jesus, but I don't need the church," or "I can worship God just as well on a hike as I can in a building."

While it's true that you can pray anywhere, the Bible knows nothing of a "solitary Christian." To follow Jesus without being part of a church is like trying to be a soldier without an army, a player without a team, or a finger without a body. In this chapter, we look at why the church isn't just a "good idea"; it's essential for your spiritual survival.

The Body of Christ: You Are a Part, Not the Whole

The most famous description of the church is found in 1 Corinthians 12, where the Apostle Paul calls it the **Body of Christ**.

Imagine a human body. It isn't just one giant eyeball or one massive foot. It is made of many parts, hands, ears, lungs, and toes, all doing different jobs.

- **The Diversity:** Every member is different. Some are "loud" parts of the body (like teachers or singers), and some are "quiet" parts (like the people who set up chairs or pray in secret).

- **The Necessity:** A hand is a wonderful thing, but if it is cut off from the body, it loses its purpose and its life. It can't do anything on its own.

- **The Unity:** If your toe gets stubbed, your whole body feels it. In the church, when one person hurts, we all hurt. When one person succeeds, we all celebrate.

The "One Anothers"

If you want to know how God expects you to live, just look at the New Testament. It contains over 50 "one another" commands.

- **Love** one another.
- **Forgive** one another.
- **Pray** for one another.
- **Encourage** one another.
- **Carry** one another's burdens.

Here is the thing: You cannot "one another" yourself. You can't practice forgiveness if you're alone in the woods. You can't carry someone's burden if you don't know anyone's problems. The church is the "gym" where we exercise our spiritual muscles. It is the place where we learn to love people who are different from us, which is exactly how we grow to be like Jesus.

Protection: The Power of the Flock

The Bible often calls God's people a "flock" and Jesus the "Great Shepherd." If you've ever watched a nature documentary, you know that predators (like lions or wolves) don't attack the center of the herd. They wait for the one sheep that thinks it knows better and wanders off on its own.

The church provides three types of protection:

1. **Safety from False Teaching:** When you are alone, it's easy to get confused by weird ideas or bad theology. In a church, you have pastors and older Christians to help you stay grounded in the truth.

2. **Safety from Temptation:** Sin grows in the dark. When we are in community, we have people who can ask us tough questions and keep us accountable.

3. **Safety from Discouragement:** Life is hard. There will be days when your faith feels weak. In those moments, the church "believes for you" until you can find your footing again.

As we learned in the last chapter, we grow through the "Means of Grace." While you can read your Bible and pray alone, there are certain things God only provides when the family gathers.

- **Corporate Worship:** There is a unique power when hundreds of people sing the same truth together. It reminds you that you are part of something much bigger than your own life.

- **The Sacraments:** Baptism and Communion (The Lord's Supper) are "visible words." They are physical reminders of what Jesus did. When we take communion together, we are reminded that we are all equal at the foot of the cross.

- **Preaching:** There is a difference between reading a book and hearing a message "live" that is directed at your community. God uses the preaching of His Word to challenge us in ways we might avoid when reading on our own.

Wait, What About the Hypocrites?

One of the biggest reasons teens avoid church is because they've seen people act like hypocrites. Maybe you've seen a leader fall into sin, or you've been judged by someone in the pews.

It's important to remember: The church is not a museum for saints; it's a **hospital for sinners**. You don't go to a hospital and get mad because there are sick people there; that's why they are there! Every person in your church, including the pastor, is a "work in progress." If the church were perfect, they wouldn't let you or me in! We stay in the church not because the people are perfect, but because the Savior is.

> "And let us consider how we may spur one another on toward love and good deeds, 25 not giving up meeting together, as some are in the habit of doing, but encouraging one another—and all the more as you see the Day approaching." - *Hebrews 10:24-25*

1. You Have a Job to Do The church is missing a piece if you aren't there. You have a specific gift, a specific personality, and a specific story that the rest of the body needs. You aren't just there to "consume" a service like you're watching Netflix; you are there to contribute.

2. You Get a Multi-Generational Perspective In school, you spend all day with people your own age. In the church, you get to talk to people who have been following Jesus for 50 years. They have wisdom you don't have yet. You also get to help those younger than you. This "family" structure keeps you from being stuck in your own little bubble.

3. It Prepares You for Heaven Heaven isn't going to be a bunch of people sitting on private clouds. It's going to be a "great multitude from every nation, tribe, and tongue" worshiping together. The church is "Basic Training" for heaven. We are learning how to live in community now so we can enjoy it forever.

1. If the church is a "Body," which part do you feel like you are? Are you a "hand" (helping), a "mouth" (encouraging), or "feet" (going)?

2. Why do you think God chose to make us depend on other people for our spiritual growth instead of just letting us grow on our own?

3. How does thinking of the church as a "hospital" change how you feel when you see someone at church act in a way that isn't like Jesus?

CHAPTER 16

BAPTISM AND THE LORD'S SUPPER

Imagine you are watching a wedding. You see the bride and groom exchange rings. Does the ring *make* them married? Not exactly. They are married because of the vows they made and the legal covenant they signed. However, the ring is a visible sign of that invisible promise. It tells the world who they belong to, and it reminds them of their commitment every time they look at it.

In theology, we call Baptism and the Lord's Supper **Ordinances** (because Jesus *ordained* or commanded them) or **Sacraments**. They are "visible words." They are physical actions, using water, bread, and juice, that act as a giant picture of what Jesus has done in our hearts.

Baptism: The Public Announcement

Baptism is the "starting line" of the Christian life. It is a one-time event where a believer is immersed in or washed with water in the name of the Father, the Son, and the Holy Spirit.

What does it symbolize?

Baptism is like a reenactment of the Gospel. When a person goes under the water, it symbolizes their "death" to their old, sinful life. When they come up out of the water, it symbolizes their "resurrection" to a new life in Christ. It is a way of saying, "The old me is dead and buried; the new me lives for Jesus."

Why do we do it?

1. **Obedience:** Jesus explicitly told His followers to go and make disciples, "baptizing them in the name of the Father and of the Son and of the Holy Spirit" (Matthew 28:19).

2. **Identification:** It is like putting on a team jersey. It tells the world, the church, and the spiritual realm that you are officially "on Team Jesus."

3. **Initiation:** It is the formal way we join the local family of God (the church).

Important Note: Baptism doesn't *save* you. You aren't saved by the water; you are saved by the grace of God through faith. Baptism is the outward sign of the inward change that has already happened.

The Lord's Supper: The Family Meal

While baptism happens once, the Lord's Supper (also called Communion or the Eucharist) is something the church does over and over again. It was started by Jesus during the "Last Supper," the night before He was crucified.

The Elements

- **The Bread:** Jesus said, "This is my body, which is given for you." The bread reminds us of the physical suffering Jesus endured to pay for our sins.

- **The Cup:** Jesus said, "This cup... is the new covenant in my blood." The juice or wine reminds us that Jesus' blood was poured out to wash away our guilt.

What are we doing during Communion?

1. **Look Back (Remembrance):** We remember the historical fact of the cross. We don't let the sacrifice of Jesus become "old news."

2. **Look In (Examination):** The Bible tells us to check our hearts before we eat. We confess any recent sins and ask God to help us live for Him.

3. **Look Around (Unity):** We eat from the same loaf and drink from the same cup to show that we are one family. There is no "VIP section" at the Lord's Table.

4. **Look Forward (Hope):** Jesus said He wouldn't drink of the fruit of the vine again until the Kingdom comes. Every time we take communion, we are practicing for the "Great Banquet" in heaven.

    "For whenever you eat this bread and drink this cup, you proclaim the Lord's death until he comes." - 1 Corinthians 11:26

You might think, "Why do we need physical stuff? Can't I just think about Jesus in my head?"

God created us with bodies, not just floating brains. He knows that we are forgetful people. He gave us baptism and the Lord's Supper because He wanted us to **see, touch, and taste** the Gospel.

- **Water** reminds us we are clean.
- **Bread** reminds us we are sustained.
- **Wine/Juice** reminds us we are forgiven.

These aren't just empty traditions. When the church gathers to perform these actions, the Holy Spirit works in a special way to nourish our faith and strengthen our bond with each other.

Why This Matters to You

1. It Gives You a "Moment to Point To" There will be days when you feel like a "fake" Christian or you doubt if God really loves you. On those days, you can look back at your baptism. It was a physical, public fact. It serves as an anchor for your soul.

2. It Keeps Your Heart Soft Taking the Lord's Supper regularly forces you to stop and deal with your sin. It's like a weekly "system restart." You can't stay mad at a brother or sister in Christ when you are both kneeling at the same table, receiving the same mercy.

3. It Connects You to History When you take the bread and the cup, you are doing the exact same thing that Christians have done in secret caves, massive cathedrals, and jungle villages for 2,000 years. You are part of an ancient, global family.

Reflect and Talk

1. If baptism is like a "wedding ring," what happens if someone wears the ring but doesn't actually love their spouse? (What happens if someone gets baptized but doesn't actually follow Jesus?)

2. Why do you think Jesus chose *food* (bread and drink) to be the way we remember Him? How is Jesus like food for our souls?

3. Have you been baptized? If not, what is holding you back from
    making that public announcement of your faith?

CHAPTER 17

TALKING TO GOD

Imagine you are friends with the most brilliant, powerful, and kind person on earth. They have given you their private phone number and told you that you can call them 24/7. They never get tired of your voice, they aren't annoyed by your "small" problems, and they have the power to actually help you with your big ones. You would probably call them all the time, right?

This is exactly what **Prayer** is. Many people think of prayer as a religious ritual, a performance, or a list of "magic words" you have to say perfectly. But at its heart, prayer is simply communication with God. It is the breath of the Christian life. If you don't breathe, you can't live. If you don't pray, your relationship with God will start to feel like a distant memory rather than a living reality.

The Purpose: Presence Over Presents

The biggest mistake we make in prayer is thinking that God is a celestial "vending machine." We put in a prayer and expect a specific "snack" to come out. If we don't get exactly what we asked for, we think the machine is broken.

But the main goal of prayer isn't to get things *from* God; it is to get **God Himself**.

- **Relationship:** Prayer is how we build intimacy with our Father.

- **Alignment:** Prayer isn't about bending God's will to match ours; it's about bending our will to match His.

- **Peace:** It is the "safety valve" for our anxiety. When we pour our hearts out to God, we trade our worries for His peace.

When Jesus' disciples asked Him how to pray, He didn't give them a lecture on theology. He gave them a pattern, often called the **Lord's Prayer** (Matthew 6:9–13). This isn't just a poem to memorize; it's a guideline we can follow for our prayers.

1. **"Our Father in heaven, hallowed be your name"**: We start by remembering who God is. He is a loving Father (intimate), but He is also in heaven (powerful). We praise Him for His character before we ask for anything.

2. **"Your kingdom come, your will be done"**: we ask that God's plans would happen in our lives, our schools, and our world. We are saying, "You're the King, not me."

3. **"Give us this day our daily bread"**: Now we ask for what we need. Note it says "daily", God wants us to depend on Him every day.

4. **"Forgive us our debts..."**: We confess our sins and ask for a clean slate. We also ask for help to forgive people who have hurt us.

5. **"Lead us not into temptation..."**: We admit we are weak and ask God to protect us from the "traps" of sin and the devil.

A Simple Tool: A.C.T.S.

If you aren't sure where to start when you close your eyes, many Christians use the acronym **A.C.T.S.** to keep their conversation balanced:

- **A - Adoration:** Tell God what you love about Him (His kindness, His power, His beauty).

- **C - Confession:** Be honest about where you've messed up today and ask for forgiveness.

- **T - Thanksgiving:** Thank Him for specific things He has done (a good grade, a fun time with friends, a sunset).

- **S - Supplication:** A fancy word for "asking." Pray for your needs and the needs of others.

Does God Always Answer?

This is the question everyone asks. The short answer is: **Yes.** But His answer isn't always "Yes."

- **Yes:** When what we ask for aligns with His perfect plan.

- **No:** When we ask for something that would hurt us or others, or doesn't fit His better plan. A good father says "no" to a child who wants to eat candy for dinner.

- **Wait:** Sometimes the timing isn't right. God uses the "wait" to grow our patience and our trust in Him.

Remember: God is a Father, not a butler. He loves you enough to give you what you *would* have asked for if you knew everything He knows.

"Do not be anxious about anything, but in every situation, by prayer and petition, with thanksgiving, present your requests to God." - *Philippians 4:6*

Why This Matters to You

1. You Have a Stress-Relief Strategy High school is stressful. Between sports, grades, social drama, and thinking about the future, it's easy to feel overwhelmed. Prayer is where you get to "unload" that baggage. You weren't designed to carry the weight of the world; God was.

2. You Are Never Truly Alone Even when you feel misunderstood by your friends or family, you have Someone who truly "gets" you. You can talk to God in the middle of a test, while you're walking to class, or in your room at night. He is the Friend who is always there.

3. It Changes You The more you talk to God, the more you start to think like Him. Your priorities shift. Things that used to make you angry start to matter less, and things God loves start to matter more. Prayer is the secret to a transformed life.

1. Why do you think we often wait until we are in a "crisis" to pray, instead of talking to God about the small things?

2. Which part of the A.C.T.S. acronym is the easiest for you? Which is the hardest?

3. How does knowing that God sometimes says "No" out of love change the way you feel when you don't get what you prayed for?

PART SEVEN

THE UNSEEN AND THE FUTURE

CHAPTER 18

ANGELS AND THE SPIRITUAL WORLD

Have you ever felt like there was more to life than just what you can see, touch, and measure? We live in a world of smartphones, concrete buildings, and biology textbooks. We are taught to trust our five senses. If we can't see it under a microscope or detect it with a telescope, we often assume it isn't there.

But the Bible pulls back the curtain on a reality that is just as real as the chair you are sitting on, yet invisible to the human eye. It tells us that we are surrounded by a spiritual realm: a world of light and darkness, of incredible beauty and intense conflict. At the center of this realm are beings created by God to serve His purposes and protect His people. We call them angels.

To understand the full story of God's Kingdom, we have to understand the "unseen" side of the universe.

What Are Angels?

The word "angel" comes from the Greek word *angelos*, which simply means "messenger." This tells us more about their **job** than their **nature**. By nature, angels are spiritual beings. They don't have physical bodies like we do, they don't get sick, and they don't die. They were created by God before the world was even formed to worship Him and carry out His commands.

1. They Are Not "Cute Babies"

In movies and art, angels are often shown as chubby babies with tiny wings or glowing ladies in white dresses. But in the Bible, when an angel appears to a human, the first thing the angel almost always has to say is: *"Do not be afraid!"* Why? Because they are terrifyingly powerful: "Praise the Lord, you his angels, you mighty ones who do his bidding, who obey his word." (Psalm 103:20). One single angel in the Old

Testament was able to defeat an entire army in one night. They are warriors, not ornaments.

2. They Are Not Human

A common misconception is that when good people die, they become angels. The Bible actually says that humans and angels are completely different "species" of creation. In fact, the Bible says that angels are fascinated by us! They "long to look" into the story of the Gospel (1 Peter 1:12). Humans are made in the image of God, and in the future, we will actually have a status that is, in some ways, higher than the angels.

3. They Are Numerous and Organized

The Bible speaks of "thousands upon thousands" and "myriads upon myriads" of angels. They aren't just a random crowd; they seem to have an order. We hear about:

- **Archangels:** Like Michael, who is described as a leader among the heavenly host.

- **Cherubim and Seraphim:** Beings that stay close to the throne of God, crying out "Holy, Holy, Holy!" Their primary job is the direct worship of God's majesty.

What Do Angels Actually Do?

Angels are not "free agents" who wander around doing whatever they want. They are perfectly obedient servants of God. Their work can be divided into four main categories:

Worshiping God

This is their favorite thing to do. In the book of Revelation, we see that the throne of God is surrounded by millions of angels who never stop praising Him. They see God's glory clearly, and their natural response is to sing about it. When we worship God in church, we are actually joining in on a "concert" that the angels have been performing for thousands of years.

Revealing God's Message

Throughout history, God has used angels to deliver big news. An angel told Abraham he would have a son. An angel told Mary she would give birth to Jesus. An angel told the shepherds in the field that the

Savior had been born. They are the "Divine Couriers" of the King.

Protecting God's People

This is where the idea of "guardian angels" comes from. While the Bible doesn't explicitly say every person has exactly one assigned angel, it *does* say that angels "encamp around those who fear him" (Psalm 34:7). Also: "Are not all angels ministering spirits sent to serve those who will inherit salvation?" (Hebrews 1:14).

Think of them as "Secret Service" agents. Most of the time, they are working behind the scenes, preventing accidents, warding off spiritual attacks, and strengthening us when we are weak. You will likely get to heaven and realize there were dozens of times an angel protected you from something you didn't even know was a threat.

Executing God's Judgment

Because angels are holy, they hate sin just as much as God does. In the Bible, we see angels used to carry out God's discipline. At the end of time, Jesus says He will send His angels to "gather out of his kingdom all causes of sin and all law-breakers" (Matthew 13:41). They are the guardians of God's justice.

The Dark Side: Fallen Angels and Spiritual Warfare

We cannot talk about the spiritual world without talking about the rebellion that happened there. The Bible tells us that at some point in the past, one of the highest angels, often called Lucifer or Satan, became proud. He didn't want to serve God; he wanted to *be* God.

He led a rebellion, and a third of the angels followed him. These are what we call **demons**.

The Nature of the Enemy

Satan and his demons are real, but we shouldn't be obsessed with them, nor should we ignore them. Here is the truth about our spiritual enemies:

- **They are defeated:** On the cross, Jesus "disarmed the spiritual rulers and authorities" (Colossians 2:15). Satan is like a lion on a leash; he can roar, but he can only go as far as God allows.

- **They are liars:** Jesus called Satan "the father of lies." Their main weapon isn't "scary movie" stuff; it is deception. They want to make you doubt God's love, doubt the Bible, and think that sin will make you happy.

- **They are temporary:** Their time is short, and they know it. Their final destination is already decided.

Spiritual Warfare

Because there is a rebellion going on, we are born into a spiritual war zone. The Apostle Paul tells us that our real fight isn't against people, our teachers, our parents, or our "enemies" at school. "For our struggle is not against flesh and blood, but against the rulers, against the authorities, against the powers of this dark world and against the spiritual forces of evil in the heavenly realms." (Ephesians 6:12)

How do we fight? We don't use physical weapons. We use the **Armor of God**:

- **The Belt of Truth:** Knowing what God says is true.
- **The Breastplate of Righteousness:** Resting in the fact that Jesus made us right with God.
- **The Shield of Faith:** Trusting God when things get hard.
- **The Sword of the Spirit:** Using the Word of God (the Bible) to fight off lies.

The Presence of the Holy Spirit vs. Angels

It is important not to get so excited about angels that we forget about the Holy Spirit. Angels are God's servants, but the Holy Spirit is God Himself.

- An angel might stand *beside* you to protect you.
- The Holy Spirit lives *inside* you to change you.

We don't pray to angels, and we don't worship them. If an angel appeared to you today and you tried to bow down, they would immediately stop you and say, "Worship God!" (Revelation 22:9). Angels are our "fellow servants." They are on our side, but they aren't our Savior.

1. You Are Never Truly Alone When you are lying in bed at night feeling scared or lonely, remember that the room isn't empty. God's "mighty ones" are stationed around you. You have a massive, invisible support system that is more powerful than any bully, any problem, or any fear you face.

2. There Is More to Your Story Than What You See Your life isn't just about grades, social media, and what you're going to do for a job. You are part of a cosmic drama. Your choices matter in the spiritual realm. When you resist temptation or pray for a friend, there is "joy in the presence of the angels of God" (Luke 15:10). You are part of a Kingdom that spans dimensions.

3. You Don't Have to Fear Evil If you've seen horror movies about demons or ghosts, it's easy to get freaked out. But for a Christian, those things have no power over you. You belong to the King of the spiritual world. "He who is in you is greater than he who is in the world" (1 John 4:4). You are on the winning side.

4. It Inspires Awe of God If the servants (angels) are this incredible, how much more incredible must the Master be? If an archangel bows his face to the ground in the presence of God , it should give us a sense of how holy and amazing our Father really is.

> "For he will command his angels concerning you to guard you in all your ways;" - *Psalm 91:11*

Reflect and Talk

1. Why do you think God chose to create an "invisible" world of angels instead of just doing everything Himself?

2. Does knowing that angels are "warriors" rather than "babies with wings" change how you feel about their protection in your life?

3. How does the reality of "Spiritual Warfare" change the way you look at the temptations or negative thoughts you have during the week?

4. If you could see the spiritual world for five minutes, what do you think would surprise you the most about your school or your home?

CHAPTER 19

WHEN JESUS RETURNS

Imagine you are watching a movie that is intense, heartbreaking, and full of suspense. The hero has been beaten down, the villains seem to be winning, and the world is in chaos. If the movie just ended there, you would leave the theater frustrated and confused. You stay in your seat because you know there is a final act. You are waiting for the moment the hero returns, sets things right, and brings peace to the story.

History is God's story, and right now, we are living in the "middle" of the book. It's a time of beauty, but also a time of great pain, sickness, and injustice. However, the Bible promises that the story does not end in a graveyard or a pile of ashes. It ends with the most spectacular event in the history of the universe: the physical, visible, and glorious return of Jesus Christ.

The Promise of the Return

When Jesus ascended into heaven forty days after His resurrection, His disciples stood staring into the sky, probably feeling a mix of awe and abandonment. Suddenly, two angels appeared: *"Men of Galilee,"* they said, *"why do you stand here looking into the sky? This same Jesus, who has been taken from you into heaven, will come back in the same way you have seen him go into heaven."* (Acts 1:11)

This wasn't a new idea. Jesus talked about His return constantly. He told His friends He was going away to "prepare a place" for them and that He would come back to get them. Throughout the New Testament, the writers mention the return of Christ over 300 times. It is the "Blessed Hope" of every Christian.

How Will He Return?

There are many different theories about the specific timeline of the "End Times" (often called **Eschatology**), but almost all Christians agree on these four facts about His coming:

1. **It will be Personal:** It won't be a "spirit" or an "influence." The same Jesus who ate fish with the disciples and has scars in His hands is the one who is coming back.

2. **It will be Visible:** It won't be a secret. Jesus said His coming would be like lightning that flashes from one end of the sky to the other. Everyone will know.

3. **It will be Sudden:** It will happen when people aren't expecting it. Jesus compared it to a "thief in the night."

4. **It will be Glorious:** The first time Jesus came, He came in a quiet stable as a weak baby. The second time He comes, He comes as the King of Kings on a white horse, surrounded by the armies of heaven.

What Will Happen When He Arrives?

The return of Jesus isn't just a grand entrance; it is the moment of ultimate "Restoration." Several massive events will take place:

1. The Resurrection of the Dead

This is one of the most incredible promises in the Bible. When Jesus returns, those who have died "in Christ" will be raised from the dead. They won't be ghosts; they will have new, physical, glorified bodies, bodies that never get sick, never age, and never die. Then, those Christians who are still alive will be transformed in an instant.

2. The Final Judgment

Jesus will settle all accounts. Every secret will be revealed, and every injustice will be addressed. For those who belong to Jesus, this isn't a day of terror, but a day of vindication. Our "Not Guilty" verdict (Justification) will be announced to the whole world. For those who rejected God, it will be the moment they are held accountable for their rebellion.

3. The Defeat of Death and Evil

The Bible says the "last enemy to be destroyed is death" (1 Corinthians 15:26). When Jesus returns, Satan, his demons, and the power of death itself will be thrown into the "lake of fire" forever. They will never be able to hurt, tempt, or destroy God's people again.

4. The New Heavens and the New Earth

God isn't going to scrap the world and start over; He is going to *fix* it. The Bible ends in Revelation 21-22 with a picture of a "New Heaven and a New Earth." It's a place where God lives with His people. There will be no more tears, no more pain, and no more goodbyes.

The "Not Yet" and the "Soon"

A question many people ask is: *If Jesus is coming back to fix everything, why is He waiting so long?*

The Apostle Peter answers this by saying that God isn't slow; He is **patient**. He is holding the door of the Kingdom open as long as possible so that more people have the chance to repent and trust Him (2 Peter 3:9). Every day that Jesus "delays" is another day of mercy for the world.

However, we are called to live in a state of "readiness." We shouldn't be so focused on "predicting" the date that we forget to live for Him today. We live with one eye on our work and one eye on the clouds.

Why This Matters to You

1. It Gives You Perspective on Suffering When you go through a hard time, a breakup, a death in the family, or a struggle with mental health, it can feel like the pain will last forever. The return of Jesus reminds you that "the best is yet to come." Your current suffering is a "chapter," but the ending of the book is joy.

2. It Gives You a Reason to Be Holy If you knew your best friend was coming over to your house in five minutes, you would probably hurry to clean up the mess in your room. Knowing Jesus could return at any moment motivates us to live lives that please Him. We want Him to find us "busy" doing His work when He arrives.

3. It Gives You a Mission If the world is going to be judged and Jesus is the only way to be saved, we have a job to do. We want to bring as many people as possible into the family before the King arrives. It turns our "boring" lives into a rescue mission.

4. It Takes Away the Fear of Death For a Christian, death isn't a "The End" sign; it's a "To Be Continued" sign. We know that even if we die before He returns, we will be raised to live in a world that is more beautiful than anything we can imagine.

> "'He will wipe every tear from their eyes. There will be no more death or mourning or crying or pain, for the old order of things has passed away." - *Revelation 21:4*

Reflect and Talk

1. If Jesus returned this afternoon, what is the first thing you would want to say to Him?

2. How does the promise of a "New Earth" (a physical world) change how you think about heaven? (Hint: It's not just sitting on clouds with harps!)

3. Why do you think God wants us to live with the "uncertainty" of when He will return, rather than giving us a specific date?

4. Who is one person in your life you want to tell about Jesus before the story ends?

CHAPTER 20

THE NEW HEAVEN AND THE NEW EARTH

If you have ever reached the final pages of a great epic novel, you know the feeling of "the bittersweet end." You've followed the characters through their darkest moments, cheered for their victories, and mourned their losses. Usually, the story ends with the hero returning home and things going back to "normal."

But the Bible doesn't end with things going back to normal. It doesn't end with us going back to the Garden of Eden. It ends with something far better: a **New Heaven and a New Earth**. This is the final destination of every person who has trusted in Jesus. It is not a place where we sit on clouds playing harps for eternity (which, let's be honest, sounds a bit boring). It is a physical, vibrant, exciting, and perfect world where we finally live life the way it was always meant to be lived.

The Great Restoration: Better Than Before

Many people think that when the world ends, God is going to destroy everything and move us to a distant, ghostly "spirit world." But the Bible uses the word *kainos*, which means "new in quality" or "renewed."

Think of it like a classic car that has been sitting in a junkyard for fifty years. It's rusted, the engine is gone, and the seats are torn. A master restorer doesn't throw the car away; he strips off the rust, replaces the broken parts, and polishes the chrome until it looks better than the day it left the factory.

That is what God is going to do with the universe. He is going to strip away the "rust" of sin, death, and decay. He is going to heal the "cracked foundation" of the earth. The result is a world that is familiar, with mountains, rivers, trees, and cities, but perfected by the presence of God.

In Revelation 21, the Apostle John gets a glimpse of this future world, and he describes it by telling us what *isn't* there. These are often called the "No Mores."

1. No More Sea

In the ancient world, the sea was a symbol of chaos, danger, and separation. When John says there is "no more sea," he isn't saying there won't be water; he's saying there will be no more chaos. The things that threaten us and keep us apart will be gone.

2. No More Death

This is the big one. We live in a world where everything dies, flowers, pets, and the people we love. In the New Earth, death is a defeated enemy. It is an extinct species. You will never have to say goodbye to a loved one ever again.

3. No More Tears or Pain

God Himself is described as leaning down to wipe away every tear from our eyes. This means that the physical pain of sickness and the emotional pain of heartbreak, anxiety, and depression will be completely healed. You won't just "forget" your old sorrows; God will settle them so perfectly that they won't hurt anymore.

4. No More Night

This doesn't mean we won't sleep; it means that the "darkness" of this world, sin, fear, and hidden evil, will have no place there. The glory of God will provide a light that never fades.

The New Jerusalem: The Ultimate City

John sees a vision of a massive city coming down out of heaven called the **New Jerusalem**. This city is the headquarters of the New Earth.

- **The Size:** The city is described as a perfect cube, roughly 1,400 miles long, wide, and high. To put that in perspective, that's about the distance from New York City to the middle of the Rocky Mountains. It is big enough for everyone.

- **The Beauty:** It is made of gold so pure it looks like glass, with walls of jasper and gates made of single pearls. This is the Bible's way of saying that the most valuable things on earth (like gold) will be so common in the New Earth that we'll walk on them like pavement.

- **The Garden-City:** In the middle of the city is the "Tree of Life" and the "River of the Water of Life." This tells us that the New Earth is a perfect blend of nature and culture. It's the best parts of a beautiful forest and the best parts of a vibrant city joined together.

What Will We Actually Do There?

One of the reasons many teens aren't excited about heaven is that they think it will be one long, never-ending church service. But the Bible suggests a much more active future.

1. We Will Work

Wait, work?! Yes, but not the kind of work that makes you tired and stressed. In the beginning, Adam and Eve were given work to do in the Garden, and it was a joy. In the New Earth, we will have projects, creativity, and responsibilities. Maybe you'll compose music, design buildings, or study the stars. You will finally have the time and the perfect brain to do what you were created to do.

2. We Will Rule

The Bible says we will "reign with Him forever and ever" (Revelation 22:5). We will be given authority to manage and care for God's creation. We are the King's children, and we will help Him run the Kingdom.

3. We Will Eat and Drink

Jesus promised that we would eat and drink at His table in the Kingdom. Imagine the best meal you've ever had, shared with the most interesting people in history, without ever feeling full or getting a stomachache. The New Earth is a place of physical pleasure and celebration.

4. We Will See His Face

This is the "Beatific Vision", the greatest reward of all. "They will see his face, and his name will be on their foreheads" (Revelation 22:4). In this life, God feels hidden or distant sometimes. In the New Earth, His presence will be as obvious as the sun. We will talk with Him, walk with Him, and know Him fully.

The "New" Body: Resurrection Life

You won't be a floating ghost in the New Earth. You will have a physical body. When Jesus rose from the dead, He had a "resurrection body." He could be touched, He could eat, and He could be recognized, but He could also travel in ways we don't understand.

- **No More Limitations:** If you have a disability, a chronic illness, or a body that you struggle to like, the New Earth offers a "software and hardware update." You will be you, but the "best" version of you, strong, healthy, and vibrant forever.

- **Recognizing Friends:** You will know your friends and family. The relationships you started on earth will continue and deepen in ways that aren't possible now.

How Do We Get There?

The most important thing about the New Jerusalem is that the gates are never shut, but "nothing impure will ever enter it" (Revelation 21:27).

This brings us back to the very beginning of our journey in this book. How can we, as sinners, enter a perfect world? The answer is only through the **Lamb of God**. Only those whose names are written in the "Lamb's Book of Life" can enter.

Jesus is the "Passover Lamb" who took our sin so that we could be clothed in His righteousness. He is the one who paid the "entry fee" for us. Heaven isn't a place for "good people"; it's a place for **forgiven people**.

Why This Matters to You

1. It Defines Your "True Home" Sometimes you might feel like you don't fit in at school or even in your own family. That's because you were made for a different world. Knowing that the New Earth is coming allows you to be "homesick for a place you've never been." It takes the pressure off this life to be perfect.

2. It Gives Value to the Here and Now If God is going to *renew* the earth rather than destroy it, then what we do now matters. The art you create, the kindness you show, and the way you care for the environment are all "previews" of the coming Kingdom. We are practicing for our forever home.

3. It Provides Absolute Hope No matter how bad your life gets, no matter how much you lose, you have a "guaranteed inheritance" that cannot be stolen or destroyed. The worst thing that can happen to you on this earth (death) is actually the doorway to the best thing that can ever happen to you.

4. It Fuels Your Mission When you realize how beautiful the New Earth is going to be, you won't want anyone to miss out. It gives you the urgency to share the Gospel with your friends. You aren't just trying to "save souls" for a ghost-world; you're inviting them to a literal, physical, eternal party.

> "He who testifies to these things says, "Yes, I am coming soon." Amen. Come, Lord Jesus". - *Revelation 22:20*

Reflect and Talk

1. If you could do one activity in the New Earth (surfing, playing an instrument, exploring a new planet) for eternity without ever getting tired, what would it be?

2. How does the idea of "No More Tears" help you when you are dealing with a hard situation right now?

3. What do you think it will be like to see Jesus' face for the first time? What is the first question you'll ask Him?

4. How does the reality of a "New Earth" make the Gospel feel more like "Good News" compared to the idea of just "going to heaven" as a ghost?

CONCLUSION

LIVING YOUR FAITH EVERY DAY

You have reached the final pages of this journey. We have traveled from the heights of the character of God to the depths of human brokenness. We have stood at the foot of the cross, peeked into the empty tomb, and looked forward to the renewal of all things in the New Heaven and the New Earth. But as you close this book, a new chapter begins—the one written by your life.

Theology is not just for libraries or classrooms; it is for the kitchen table, the locker room, the social media feed, and the quiet moments of your room. If what you believe doesn't change how you live, then you haven't truly believed it yet. Living your faith every day is the process of taking these massive truths and "putting skin on them." It is about becoming a living, breathing representative of the King in a world that is hungry for hope.

The Integration: Faith is Not a Compartment

Most people in our world live "compartmentalized" lives. They have a "school box," a "friend box," a "family box," and perhaps a "Sunday morning box." They behave differently depending on which box they are in. But the call of Jesus is a call to **integrity**. The word *integrity* comes from the same root as *integer*; it means a whole number, something that cannot be divided.

Living your faith every day means there is no "secular" part of your life. Every square inch of your existence belongs to God. Whether you are studying for a math test, playing a video game, or hanging out at the mall, you are doing it in the presence of God and for the glory of God.

The Daily Rhythm: Morning, Noon, and Night

How do we actually do this? It starts with creating a rhythm. Just as your heart has a beat and your lungs have a breath, your spiritual life needs a cadence.

1. The Morning: The Orientation

Before you check your notifications, before you look at your schedule, you must orient your heart. This is the time to remind yourself of who you are. You are a child of God, adopted by grace, and empowered by the Spirit.

- **The "Yes":** Start the day by saying "Yes" to God's will before you even know what the day holds.

- **The Scripture:** Read even just a few verses to set the "tone" for your mind. Let God's voice be the first one you hear.

2. The Noon: The Alignment

The middle of the day is usually when the "flesh" starts to take over. You're tired, someone was rude to you, or you're stressed about a deadline. This is the time for "breath prayers." A simple, five-second prayer like, *"Lord, give me your patience right now,"* or *"Father, remind me that you are with me,"* can realign your soul in the middle of the chaos.

3. The Night: The Examination

Before you sleep, practice the "Examen." This is an ancient way of looking back at the day with God.

- **Gratitude:** What were the "grace moments" today? Where did you see God working?
- **Confession:** Where did you stumble? Don't hide it; bring it to the light, receive forgiveness, and leave it at the foot of the cross.
- **Trust:** Hand the day back to God. You can sleep because He never does.

Faith in the Classroom: The Mystery of Stewardship

For most of you, "work" is school. You might think that math, history, or science have nothing to do with your faith, but that couldn't be further from the truth.

If God created the world, then every subject you study is an exploration of His handiwork.

- **Science** is the study of how God organized the physical world.
- **Math** is the study of the logic and order God built into the universe.
- **History** is the story of God's providence and human nature.
- **Art and Literature** are expressions of the creativity God placed in us because we are made in His image.

When you work hard in school, you aren't just doing it for a grade or to get into a good college; you are doing it as an act of worship. Excellence is a way of saying "Thank You" to God for the brain He gave you. Integrity in school means not cheating—not because you're afraid of getting caught, but because you know that God sees your heart and values truth more than a GPA.

The Challenge of Secular Education

In many classrooms, God is left out of the conversation. You might feel like you have to check your faith at the door. But a robust theology allows you to engage with secular ideas without being swept away by them. You can learn from the brilliance of secular thinkers while filtering their ideas through the lens of Scripture. When you encounter ideas that contradict God's Word, you don't have to be angry; you can be curious and prayerful, asking the Holy Spirit to help you see where the truth has been twisted.

Your friends are the people who will see your faith most clearly. You don't necessarily have to "preach" at them every day. In fact, sometimes the best witness is simply being a different kind of friend.

1. The Gossip-Stopper

In a world where everyone talks behind everyone's back, a person who refuses to participate in gossip stands out like a neon light. When you choose to speak well of others or simply remain silent when others are being torn down, you are reflecting the heart of a God who is Truth and Love.

2. The Listener

Everyone wants to be heard, but few people truly listen. Because you have a Father who listens to you, you can afford to be the friend who listens to others. Sometimes, "living your faith" just looks like sitting with a friend who is crying and not trying to "fix" them with a clichéd Bible verse, but just being there because Jesus is "with us" in our pain.

3. The Forgiver

Conflict is inevitable. But while the world holds grudges and cancels people, the Christian has a superpower: Forgiveness. When you are the first one to say, "I'm sorry," or the first one to say, "I forgive you," you are putting the Gospel on display. You are showing them what Jesus did for you.

We cannot talk about daily life without talking about your digital life. Your phone is perhaps the place where your faith is most tested.

The Trap of Comparison

Social media is designed to make you feel "less than." It shows you the highlight reels of everyone else's life while you are living your "behind-the-scenes." Living your faith means finding your identity in what God says about you, not in how many likes or views you get. Before you post, ask yourself: *Am I doing this to be noticed, or am I doing this to be helpful?*

The Power of the Tongue (and the Thumb)

The Bible warns us that the tongue can set a whole forest on fire (James 3). Today, that "tongue" is often our keyboard. Before you leave a comment or share a post, ask: *Is this true? Is this kind? Is this necessary?* A Christian's digital footprint should be one of peace, not outrage.

The Hard Days: When Faith Feels Dry

There will be days, sometimes weeks or months, where you don't "feel" God. You'll read your Bible and it will feel like reading a phone book. You'll pray and it will feel like the words are hitting the ceiling.

This is normal. Faith is not a feeling; it is a commitment. Just as a pilot flies by the instruments when they can't see through the clouds, we live by the "instruments" of God's Word when we can't see His hand.

- **Keep Showing Up:** Don't stop praying just because you don't feel "goosebumps."
- **Lean on the Family:** This is why you need the church. When your faith is weak, you can lean on the faith of others.
- **Look Back:** Remind yourself of what God has done in the past. If He was faithful then, He is faithful now, even in the "dark."

The Dark Night of the Soul

Theologians sometimes call these periods of dryness the "dark night of the soul." It isn't necessarily a sign of sin; it's often a sign of growth. God is teaching you to love Him for who He is, not just for the "spiritual high" He gives you. When you keep choosing God even when it feels hard, your faith is being refined into something much stronger and more beautiful than a mere feeling.

Developing a Christian Worldview

Living your faith every day means developing a "Christian Worldview." This is the lens through which you see everything. A worldview answers the four biggest questions of life:

1. **Origin:** Where did I come from? (Creation)
2. **Meaning:** Why am I here? (Imago Dei and Glory)

3. **Morality:** What is wrong with the world? (Fall)
4. **Destiny:** Where is everything going? (Redemption and Restoration)

When you watch a movie, listen to a song, or read a news article, you should be asking: *What is this telling me about these four questions?* If a movie tells you that you are just a collection of chemicals with no purpose, your worldview allows you to say, "I know that's not true because I am made in the image of God." Living your faith means being an active thinker, not a passive consumer.

The Theology of the Mundane

One of the most radical things you can learn as a young Christian is that God cares about the "boring" parts of your day. We often look for God in the "big" moments, the mountain-top retreats, the emotional youth group nights, or the answered miracles. But God is just as present when you are washing the dishes, walking the dog, or sitting in traffic.

The Apostle Paul tells us, *"Whatever you do, work at it with all your heart, as working for the Lord, not for human masters,"* (Colossians 3:23). This means there is no such thing as a "useless" task if it is done for God. When you do your chores with a good attitude, you are serving Christ. When you take care of your body through exercise and rest, you are honoring the temple of the Holy Spirit. This "theology of the mundane" turns your entire life into an ongoing act of worship.

The Stewardship of Time and Talents

God has given you a unique set of gifts, personality traits, and a specific amount of time. Living your faith means being a good "steward" of these resources. Stewardship isn't just about money; it's about managing everything God has put in your hands.

Identifying Your Gifts

You might be good at art, or sports, or explaining complex things, or making people laugh. These aren't just "talents"; they are gifts from the Spirit meant to be used for the good of others. Ask yourself: *How can I use my skill in [blank] to bless someone else this week?*

Prioritizing Your Time

Time is the most limited resource you have. In a world full of distractions, living your faith means being intentional. It doesn't mean you can never watch Netflix or play games, but it means those things shouldn't be the center of your world. It means making time for the things that last forever: your relationship with God and your relationships with people.

The Battle for the Mind: Mental Health and Faith

We live in a time where many young people struggle with anxiety, depression, and mental health challenges. Living your faith does not mean you "shouldn't" struggle with these things. Faith is not a magic shield that makes life easy.

However, theology gives us a place to stand when our minds feel like they are betraying us.

- **The Truth of Your Worth:** When your brain tells you that you are worthless, the Gospel tells you that you were worth the life of the Son of God.

- **The Comfort of the Comforter:** The Holy Spirit is called the Comforter for a reason. He is with you in the panic and the darkness.

- **The Grace for Medicine and Therapy:** God has provided wisdom through doctors and therapists. Seeking help is not a lack of faith; it is a stewardship of the brain God gave you.

Living your faith in the midst of mental health struggles means being honest about your pain while clinging to the hope that your "feelings" aren't the ultimate truth—God's Word is.

Living as a Resurrected Person

Living your faith every day means living as a "resurrected person." This means you no longer have to live as a slave to your old habits.

If you struggled with a quick temper, you aren't "just an angry person" anymore. You are a new creation. You have the power of the Spirit to choose a different path. This doesn't happen all at once (that's Sanctification), but it starts with a change in identity. You don't "try" to be good to get God's love; you "act" like who you already are, a beloved child of the King.

The Great Commission: Your Role in the Big Story

As we conclude, remember that your life is not just about your own personal growth. You have been drafted into a mission. Before Jesus left, He gave us the **Great Commission**: *"Therefore go and make disciples of all nations, baptizing them in the name of the Father and of the Son and of the Holy Spirit,"* (Matthew 28:19).

This sounds intimidating, but it starts in your daily life.

- **Identify:** Who has God placed in your life who doesn't know Him? Your lab partner? Your teammate? Your sibling?

- **Invest:** How can you serve them and love them? Sometimes the best way to share the Gospel is to be the only person who actually cares about their life.

- **Invite:** When the time is right, can you tell them the story of the King who rescued you? You don't need all the answers; you just need to share what you've seen and heard.

You are an ambassador. Everywhere you go, from the coffee shop to the classroom, you are representing a different Kingdom. You are a scout for the New Earth, showing people a "preview" of what is to come through your joy, your hope, and your love.

The Final Charge: Stay the Course

Theology is meant to lead to doxology (praise). All this knowledge about God should make you love Him more. This book was never intended to just fill your head with facts; it was intended to set your heart on fire.

Don't be afraid of the journey ahead. You have the Word of God as your map, the Holy Spirit as your power, and the Church as your traveling companions. And most importantly, you have a Savior who has promised: *"and teaching them to obey everything I have commanded you. And surely I am with you always, to the very end of the age."* (Matthew 28:20).

There will be moments when you want to give up. There will be seasons where the world seems too loud and God seems too quiet. In those moments, remember the empty tomb. Remember that the same power that conquered death is currently at work in you.

Go out into the world. Be bold in your convictions. Be humble in your interactions. Be kind to the broken. Live like someone who has been rescued, because you have. Live like someone who is going to live forever, because you are.

A Final Prayer for the Reader

Heavenly Father,

I thank you for the person reading these words right now. I thank you that they are not an accident, but a masterpiece created by You for a specific purpose in this generation. You knew them before the foundation of the world, and You have called them by name.

Lord, I pray that the truths in this book would move from their head to their heart, and from their heart to their hands. May they not just be "hearers" of the Word, but "doers." When they feel weak, remind them of Your strength. When they feel lonely, remind them of Your presence. When they feel like a failure, remind them of Your grace which is new every morning.

Give them the courage to stand for truth in a world that often calls evil good and good evil. Give them the compassion to love the unlovable and to see people as You see them. Help them to see their school, their home, and their future through the lens of Your Kingdom.

May their life be a "thank you" note to You for all You have done. May they grow in the knowledge of Jesus Christ and bear fruit that lasts. We look forward with joy to the day we see You face to face and hear the words, "Well done, good and faithful servant."

Until then, help us to run the race with endurance, looking to Jesus, the founder and perfecter of our faith.

In the name of Jesus, the King of Kings and Lord of Lords, Amen.

www.ingramcontent.com/pod-product-compliance
Lightning Source LLC
Chambersburg PA
CBHW060636080726
47818CB00004B/162